.

IMMOBILITY

--POETRY

Iván Argüelles

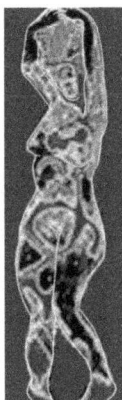

2022
LUNA BISONTE PRODS

IMMOBILITY
-- POETRY

(Written 07-07-2021 to 10-25-2021)

"el deber del Poeta es
convertir el Paraíso en Infierno"
Roberto Bolaño, Sepulcros de Vaqueros

A mis muertos de cada día:
a mi hijo Max, a mi hermano Joe,
y a tantos otros con o sin nombre.

Back cover photo by Raymond Holbert
Cover art, illustrations, book design by C. Mehrl Bennett

ISBN 9781938521829

https://www.lulu.com/spotlight/lunabisonteprods

LBP

Luna Bisonte Prods
137 Leland Ave
Columbus OH 43214 USA

SATURDAY AFTERNOON AT THE MOVIES

how can we recuperate what we saw on the screen
both of us peering deep into the fault-line of infinity
when two is only the multiple of one the self without
its mask the pronoun of indivisibility and oblivion
what was ever achieved looking on the other side
where squads of angels lacking total recall
cluster around the fever-point turning inside out
and speaking to us through megaphones of fists
warned us not to go further east where copies of
the solar homophone prepare to destroy the sky
all memory is poured into a siphon leaving us void
empty figures to whom no shadows belong static
in our perception that we are the center of nowhere
silhouettes in a camera-eye that transfigures night
and the countless unnamed celestial bodies into
mere negatives shapeless unimaginable content
both of us on the border separating space from time
playing with figures drawn from the origins of sleep
the size of the mind ! illusion of existence *and* death
puppets of thought toys and maps lucid imitations
creating and erasing experiences in an instant
and call that living ! commerce of glass and mirage
to stop on the first step and invent cigarettes and
booze the stammering practice of impersonation
teenage impostors irreverent dialects hills !
the rapture of statues in their perfect instability
to eternalize noon irreversible instant of recognition
we were *there* looking at the person in the coffin
it was no one if not you or I mistaken corollaries
of ourselves zygotes ruminant spermatozoa
specks of amnesia and longing in perpetuity
walking the Logos like a twelve-bar blues
understanding nothing of the algebra of breath
two and two always just one on the finite dot
disregarding the daily toss of the I Ching
the supplication to bonzes burned in defiance
of the laws of warfare and peace the virtual
assessment of the time remaining before the Bust
cops and drug-traffickers trading egos

in the airport bar three in the morning when
Saint John of the Cross in hallucinatory tuxedo
stands to read the poem called *The Great Crossing*
nothing is stable in this very instant of transformation
visionary duplicates and hiatus of cosmic cessation
I am the punctuation intended to define *you* !
neither of us anywhere in sight a pair of kids
scared to go home sitting in a dark movie theater
waiting for the horse to come around the bend
this time without its rider

07-07-21

THE BOTTOM OF THE SWIMMING POOL

*Chi è costui che senza morte
va per lo regno della morta gente?*

always the same month day hour minute week
muffled cries and shouts from the diving board
barely reach the tar-patched concrete bottom
body parts red cloth coverings the eight thousand
girls born on the same day as the Buddha all
here in two piece swim-suits eyes and voices like
a radio that can't be turned off the famous sky
one remove from death looming menacingly low
the intimations and warnings of a finality in
the soundless echoes booming from life-guards
bronzed like unrecognized deities perched on
canvas chairs overlooking the escape routes
to Shangri-La and the seven nether levels below
the Himalayas where the fates design forgeries
of illegible poetry attached to eyes opened
forever underwater and the surprise waking
to a borrowed daylight fusion of jazz and grass
everything akimbo immensely silent mirrors
in reverse upside down as the cosmos really is
playing Medusa with Friday night's date
sixty fathoms under where diving bells grow
loud and incandescent with insane love lyrics

2

a chrysalis of pure sand bursting in the ears
and a red light that says the holiday's over
neon goldfish satellites of the moon weaving
through the phantoms of drowned planets
the ominous copies of rebirths and deaths
jingle ringing of unseen musical instruments
slash and plunge of corpses looking for breath
in the plangent expired depths of summer
hands tingling for an inch of future and mouths
opened to the eventualities of kissing the Mystery
coming up for air lungs like exaggerated drums
the world returns with its deadly black sun
afloat belly up on the surf of the galactic sea
in an instant the overwhelming absence of eternity
sets the vivid phenomena of hue and sound
spinning phantasmagoria of memory and dreams
together in a blurred photographic time-lapse
when the multiple pronouns of oblivion *speak* !
as if night had turned itself into an infinite day
when the gorgeous zombies of adolescence spent
whole afternoons in the subaquatic secrets
learning nothing and forgetting everything

07-08-21

THE BAFFLEMENT

the universe is a prisoner of mind !
language is a tumult of noise without echoes
no one says anything without dying first
in the graveyard of thought and when it's over
and the galaxies are plunging in reverse
and phenomena of matter are still-born
on the photographic negative what's to say ?
statues have their fill of sound and meaning
noon is the spark and the lengthening shadows
the vowel that assembles the distances of light
and time and Lo to sleep in the nook where
grass has its origins and the novelty of leaves

burgeoning across the air-waves and the spokes
of the wheel and the sun itself a newborn !
the Buddha is jabbering in his saffron rag
and walking up and down the mountain
looking for the cave of eternal repose and what
a joy poetry is in its occidental hexameters
and growing up to read one day a few lines
and exclaim ! but the sadness of delight
the chrome and abuse of adolescence the motors
left running and the cavities where memory
struggles to disown itself is it a wonder
we are waiting for the Reunion and heat
blessing the circle of ideas and the fields
of sudden and emptiness yearning for wheat
to become bread and to sit around the table
not knowing who each of us is or are
eyes wide to the arc of sky and searching
insecure of hand and property for what the mind
has to teach if today is the one and success
is no measure at all we fail at knowing
in the end anything but the beauties of once
now but the sovereign mystery how it ends
the cosmos in its unreality as we are too

07-08-21

TO THE IMMOBILE GODS

not the immortality but the immobility
of the thirty-three gods noise of their renown
is all plague and theater meaningless words
what are we to them ? a tree uprooted
a defense system or the abscess of thought
many are the childhood moments of eternity
rolling down the park slope greenery before
unconscious night takes over the dim
repartition of nation states in the back brain
full text dissolved just by waking again as
butterfly or worm in the sand and vowels

flung to the winds or caught in the lace
of leaf and ivy struggling to give sound
to mind the unopened envelope of repercussion
and envy and search the trilobite for sense
and feelings the screen cannot hold back
raids of fireflies and lunar moths the dance
a particular consonant gives to experience
by daybreak to ask if the sun is nothing more
than an automatic syllable black and lethal
the rigid homophone of apparent motion
it is statues we are fixed in amnesia and loss
the excess of play and overture as breath
looking for a last escape route we call out to
the immobile and futile deities for this spare
instant of irreversible rumor if anything
can ever come back if the nodule and focus
of a buried myth the vocalic shape of memory
disguise and pronoun of the masks of dream
shadow entities of verbiage and grace phantoms
of reverie and longing islands lost in light
the turbulence of a single finger cut from
the main dizzy in the weary monopoly of grass
what a rendition of *being* ! motors of silence
the increment of space where we are tossed
asleep awake half-dead oracles of doubt
it was a minute past the end of time when
we last set the prayer wheel moving

07-09-21

THE REAWAKENING

what's the difference—eighty or three thousand years ?
sooner or later even the gods of the *unconscious* die
grass and the mutations of children's voices high
in the immobile air of eternity what can you hear ?
a flute a paradigm of noise the rush of the years
through a broken reed the nascent sun in its saddle
of quicksilver and bitumen all Hail ! language
is an imperfection marble quarried for human effigies
the combs and wattle the bruised knees and concrete
cities ! how many can exist side by side without burning
here was a stump stricken by lightning and there
on the road's third margin the trees of infinite sorrow
where winters dwell in dead hives longing for a taste
it is a disease to wake and walk again and swell
the mirrors with the adder of pride and summon
from the depths of night mantras of recall and dying
how much effort in the thumbnail ! deserts and islands
the plangent sense of humans toiling to make a shape
and to alert the skies about the flight and fall of planets
why did we ever give them names ? step aside it is
a moment of silence for the commonly buried for
urging of inconstancy for the mind to come forth
for what it is an embattled insect with a foreign accent
listen to the radio ! it is almost never the day you think
nor in the transparent grammar of memory the summer
or the water or even the dust we must endure lying
abed with a breathless heat dazed and delirious
I know *that* ! I am *that* ! and lapse like a stained leaf
into the passing breeze forever the longing for form
the impossibility of being duplicate a copy a mere
vessel for sound and the heightened loss of awareness
consonants of the ring sliding from use a hand
that grasps for itself but not its other what a maze !
it can happen always when least expected the trained
eye fixed inward waiting for the syllable of light
the ear that darkens in its ultimate lunation
mountains ! soon the accident of the future sleep
the gravel and the wheel that cannot return
the window !

07-09-21

6

AN ELEGY :

the exact moment when the body decides
or the fiction of the soul wending sky-ward
a bliss to have shed leaf and twig raiment
of earthly brevity the clouds in the their *hapax
legomenon* dot the atmospheres with a fatal
punctuation of never again and a finger
somewhere in the below of memory goes
on its own through darkening seas of grass
a lone butterfly bearing the dust of eons on
its transparent tinted wings aflutter eyeing
the solar homophone signals a complex code
of immortality's short-lived hour and vanishes
a blur of hues in no one's recollection and what
of the endeavor to classify and record
sounds and depictions of noise the syntax
of communication between statues or the grand
perplexity of humans to erect monuments to
the mind's staggering failures in porous rock
or pages of limestone and asbestos entire
histories of snail and curlew mythologies
that create gods out of the gravel and water
that runs down into the famous grottos
where they say Eurydice still wanders dazed
in the broken promise of light and shade
we are here at once then are *not* a futility
of illusion deception and repercussion
remembering a time when eternity was
the imminent fraction of time when amazed
we recognized then forgot *what* we recognized
and went on playing on swings and slides
in the park that exists just outside
the House of phantomatic absences

07-10-21

THE DESTROYED WORK OF PHILIP LAMANTIA

the unspeakable poem a lesion in the faint air
winnowing around the leaf the *what* can never
be said or memorized nor written on the conscious
brow intimations of a former life the being and
existence of unrecorded sound the levity and breadth
of a censored thought the vagabond brain with its
copies of Rimbaud and Baudelaire resonance of
a brittle century the futile orient of inspiration
grounding a note in the broken reed and playing
each finger an octave higher than the last brim
with those hell-goers who themselves betrayed
bone and oracle of imperfection sense and noise
the colossal vowel that destroys everything and
let the sun busy its wake in the shattered lamp
and hooves echo sparking the celestial cement
we are fictions with parasols made of eyelids
and dance the ferried consonant of eternity
into its midnight abscess deed and function to
honor the dead the conduits of memory the frail
non-consequence of breath here on the other side
plateaus of nasturtium and regret bonzes playing
fire against fire in the tumultuous extra month
predicted by Orpheus floating downstream his
head the immense gravity the shell the void
and hollow of the train of verses ricocheting in
the quarry where stone-cutters carve destinies out
of living rock assigning name and pronoun to shapes
like unto Venus and Daphne the fluid ornaments
of mythical paralysis the aphasia and breakdown
of the nerve the fossil tongue the blinded pupil
the cataract and pornography of mental progress
the worm distilled from smoke rising from number Three
dichotomies of insane privilege bedlam and sweat-shop
spinal refractions the impulse to alcohol and drugs
righteous nonsense the abstract painting of Mind
and et cetera the recitation in the weapons depot
of the famous poetries of India and Spain and Lorca
against the wall riddled with bullets of silver shadow
whose fist does not anger at these obscenities ?
poetry ! the give and take of an empty body a world
outside the world a quake inside the thinking knee

to proceed the fractured inch and require the moon
to undress its ropes and plunge !

07-10-21

THE LIFE THAT COMES AND GOES

rebel heart they say of all the children gone
the twelve or thirteen steps it takes to cross
to the other side a page reversed a tumbler
of water spilled the temperature too high
to count the fever blister in the mouth the acid
corroding the inch of air required to breathe
histories of tide and surf that cliffs cannot abide
the world's smallest version is but an ink-blot
and the pool where spotted deer come to drink
the park where Buddha laid his shadow down
and trees that grace the entrance to the sky
their lush foliage an instant then withered dry
there is no truth to tell no eternity to endure
the tiny spots that besiege the moon the noise
that ravels within the ear a repercussion to hear
a dozen and more the suns that rise in a second
before surrendering horse and rider on the wire
down plunge the angry planets and swoop from
underneath the oceans monsters with pronouns
that resonate like gold against the porcelain of echo
which day infinite and wild is this heated by what
the mind suffers in its infantile confusion to
apprehend darkness and the grass that grieves
every other minute in sounds broken by
marble and aphasia playing with a plastic toy
a vowel too fast to recall and fiercely cloying
consonants that alter language at the base
the accident of life ! the storefronts boarded up
the traffic stopped at the bridge the schoolyards
ghosted by all the children gone unnoticed until
too late and evening takes by surprise the knees
the bruised and fragile skin the hair unkempt and
shirts on backwards and heaven in the comb
phone-calls

that invent sorrow in the night
too much and so little !

07-11-21

THREE NEW SONNETS

SONNET PASSING

a hair a hue a hint of one's reflection
the thunder of the years has passed and
now the ruffled claim of a borrowed echo
the repercussion and resonance of sleep
to come the inert and quasi-moving leaf
that seems to copy distances where wind dies
and the solitary rock that parts the way
between what has been and what can never be
shifts ever so slightly in its darkened space
alone beside the unlit window listening
with cupped hand for the gravel and night
with its thousand tiny deities the fireflies
gone the dubious lamp of day the shade
of vanishing vowels the very sound of time

SONNET ASKING

my wounded mind is it a stone or a petal?
at what level of consciousness do I exist ?
there is no road map no hand no arrow
to guide this patched copy of thought out
of the labyrinth of memory and obsession
am I a taper flickering at the entrance to hell
or merely a leaf exhausted by the sound of
its own voice darkening in green echoes ?
if I turn to glass does it reflect a pronoun
stained by ink and smoke worn from use
or if I drop like a rock into passing waters
do the fish who dart like lightning care ?

how many is the number it takes to climb ?
is this the silence that marks the end of time ?

SONNET HOMERIC

the poem that Homer wrote forty years ago
the Helen he claimed was only substance a noun
declined for gender and number and Ajax
like a hero meant to grovel in the dust and die
mere sounds that echo in the ear's forged panoply
legends carved out of a metamorphosis of mind
the trivial transport ships with colored sails
the angry winds and rocks that flail all night
the brooding and clipped wings of fate that burn
this poem was meant to relay all that and the end
of things that dream and sleep forevermore
in the grassy limbs of ancient heavens gone
transept and flux of deathless repercussion and
gods cut out of early paper and lost to memory

07-12-21

BE A TROUBADOUR!
Ab Flamenca, ma dóuz'amía

be a troubadour ! sing and buzz and hum
speak in ancient dialects of honey-comb and thorn
fill the interstices of your sounds with eglantine
and wear laurel and musk and yearn pining
for the unnamed *Lady of Tripoli* who lives in dreams
on your palfrey alone journey towards the hills
where Ovid's ghost wrapped in tatterdemalion
spooks crumbling tombstones with archaic verse
from lords of distance and cloud the Saracens
steal what you can understand of their lyric tropes
who better than you to imitate Orlando in his madness
for Angelica naked on a rock like a statue but
for her waving hair all gold in the resonance
of the late medieval sun of black homophones

and melancholy and evening find you outside of time
no inn has doors wide enough nor stables deep
with mysteries of the *Beloved* of Ramon Llull
for you to find a place to sleep and fret and
tune the chords of your broken music and shout !
anger too befits your heresy *Cathar* and vagabond
dualistic frame of mind and moons and planets
that burn at noon like satellites of language
put to the pyre of dogma and misunderstanding
be a troubadour ! sing and buzz and hum
be as the dust of time the mists and holy rocks
and pools so dark and dense with lotus and pearl
the disappearance of all noise and colored air
is yours alone the head you lay beneath the stone
the soul you bury in the fragrant hollyhock

07-12-21

NIBBANA

in the coffin where I lay
my dream was to return one day
with beads and spangles that queens wear
and dice tossed carelessly in a rout
the life we seem to share is no more than
a spider's span a butterfly's brief display
of hue and flight and distances painted
on the sleeping eye and what if waking
were just as much a slight as the nerve
that snaps or the shoulder's grief
we come and go through mirrors braiding
hair or fastening buckles to some cloth
what is memory but the partial light
of a fleeting hour the dense knot of consonants
or intricacies of vowels lingering in the ear
the remote jabber in the mind of sounds
and noises little more than symphonies of crickets
or the fading shapes of words locked in a lexicon
at day's end who can say of the thousand minutes
which was the most important one ?

a Buddha will pass through the afternoon
a parasol and begging cup in his hands
the quiver of a faint smile the agony of
recall and doubt the film unraveling in his mind
a birth before and a death afterwards the narration
of constant repetition the thunder and elation
of the momentary eternity when a deer
came to feed from his yellow palms
the end was yesterday the incomplete moment
spark and smoke that filled the air
a tree a lawn insects that rule the earth
placed his head upon deathless stone
and as the cosmos of a million universes
came to rest upon a single leaf above
the child he had been // a lingering evening shout
dissolved in the fire that is no more

07-13-21

DANGERS OF BOYHOOD

I was a boy once who played with ricocheting
sounds rubber balls and telescopes
and watched cyanide-colored clouds flood
the air as sky separated from itself
in the constant puzzle of wondering *why*
was a boy no more than memory can allow
a growing tide of cells and wayward hair
hands that learned to untie knots
and fasten to the winds a longing for
who knows *what* a clutter of vowels
and noisy syllables and stammered
many a wordless epithet against the breeze
the rumors of language the order of tones
accents screwed to syntax and legends
of cliffs that yelled and roaring rocks
tossed into a seething sea where
nymphs and mermaids tortured souls

and poets clamored for surprise
fingers wrote strange names on bark
and paper planes sent messages to the gods
a creation of light and circumflex a script
between the ears that yearned for a past
history came and went with the hummingbird
and gaps of time were filled by butterflies
still alone I remained a boy to this very day
I seemed to love sometimes for weeks on end
and sustained grief the hurt of loss
and lingering the knowledge of never more
eternity was the dew that clings to the leaf
infinity the number I could not count
each day was just like the one before
and death the note pinned to the door

07-13-21

THE HOME-COMING QUEEN EURYDICE

though I saw her crying profusely
I knew she was dead
though poetry has much power
it cannot bring back the dead
it cannot generate a new rebirth
it is not a magic science of thought-reading
it cannot be recited in the language of the Sanskrit-twin
poetry does not subscribe to the descent of idioms
nor to the confusion of tongues
poetry is as much aphasia as amnesia
yet I saw her bawling her eyes out
and I knew she was more dead than space
nor can poetry turn lions into stone
it is at best an activity of cloud physics
nor can it be Latin and Tuscan at the same time
promising hierarchies of sainthood and demonology
poetry is not metaphysics nor algebra nor even a civil war cannon
leaning on an invisible hemisphere she was listening to music
no one else could hear the sound of sea-anemones

poetry is neither vertigo nor the unconscious struggling for light
though poetry is capable of great things
of causing rocks and trees to grieve
and to bring down from the heavens the scourge of planets
turning noon into an infinite marble quarry
from which statues are given speech acts
to mourn and lament the passing day
it cannot be at the square root of number
nor take on wings and fly to the molten sun
the great blackening asterisk that guides
still she kept weeping so loud and plaintive
I could not bear her death nor the song
that no one else could hear
poetry cannot take the knees in supplication
to re-write what it could not write in the first place
sarcophagus and milestone marker of the indivisible
poetry has a task it can never accomplish
sitting on the bottom rung of the infernal ladder
poetry is just the beginning of smoke and ash
and her tears which were in the millions flooded
the small field where the football players gathered
to salute the blind Mystery of coming and going
though it was a dream and her intense sorrowing
the overflow of her pain the unbearable
yet she was dead more dead than the naked goddesses
who are wont to parade in a film before mortals
I then recognized who she was--the homecoming queen
Eurydice crowned just minutes earlier
given to believe she would regain the lamp of day
only to be felled by a backwards glance

07-14-21

AN ACCOUNT OF MY FIRST MEETING
WITH POET NEELI CHERKOVSKI

at the Bateau-Ivre in the year of our domino
nine thousand ninety nine and the hundred demons
of perplexity and divinity the sooth in his eyes

struggling shadows of Lorca-communism in his wake
the poet the poet Neeli Cherkovski a subterfuge of rage
and quiet ash a buddhahood of immemorial shapes
Bixby Canyon San Bernardino topographies ready to burn
or done in by jihad terrorists with eyes of faun and doe
no longer smoking but lounge in the lobbies of hotels
defamed by asterisks where he must have slept
before coming to this our first encounter a brooding
music of Thelonious and Bird off tuned piano & sax
crystallized by nights spent with Kaufman or Bukowski
a Japanese script illegible as his hands slowly turning
crimson like Grant Avenue three AM yet somehow
an afternoon only Debussy could paint evoking a
thought only a thought of poet Mallarmé and
as a refuge from the errors of time and space Lunch
steaming French onion soup and salmon on the side
neat white napkins exploding silently like galaxies
between the forged silverware a poet Neeli a poetry
unraveling like cocktail noise will soon to be a third rail
death is not a stranger but the waiter bending politely
the Proustian enigma of his face patiently taking orders
to suicide or not to suicide outside a dog expects
His Master to retrieve him from a locked automobile
and maybe a bone text to rival the early Chinese bonzes
drunk on a sliver of moonlight like poet Neeli reverie
and I will politely recommend a flagon of Homeric white
imitation of Lesbos or Capri as the vagaries of a plan
a poetry book a volume called *Animal* emerges in
the context of dead beatniks and Mayakovsky or two
he will be gentle an aspirin shaped planet dissolving in his grin
shaggy poet Neeli our first encounter summoning up
Rimbaud and all eighteen year old devotees of Krishna
saffron hued in their imperfect dance of the tombstones
asphodel for dessert or the holy moly of a waxen Ulysses
tied to the raft of danger which is the way poetry is headed
demolition of the senses the divine interplay of sound
and language meaningless as all eternities are

07-14-21

CONFESSION IN A HIATUS

can I take myself seriously really ? is this a poet
a pocket full of nonsense the idea the past is now
the future nothing to gain a person but a mask
an uneven flow of syllables on a trajectory toward
the void memory a riddled piece of stone a sieve
through which flow all manner of hues and noise
the brain's a mill-wheel run down creaking and
out of sorts like the eye that wanders sleepless
across the target of the skies asterisk and bee-hive
junction of error and rumor obsession and desire
the lust to play forever adolescent games of love
troubadour of mimicry vestigial echoes of self
proud one minute dejected for lack of recognition
loosely fit in skin of parable and parody the ego
self-formed minute insect crawling trying to fly
winged absences and loves gone wrong the fix
in the arm and walkabout passions rhyming
misgiven thoughts about the *this* and the *that*
and always the doubt and grief the sorrow and
penance pentimento and imitation of store-bought
ideas pausing to adjust the glass to reflect back
the quixotic countenance of the Homeric-be-alike
penning misquoted origins of the first line of
all poems the one and single madness of breath
to exude confidence and set to music the vast
and unwritten text the invisible ink of promise
it'll be finished tomorrow it will go to the moon
with Angelica it will be a spoon and a monitor a
ringing device to remind the sleeper that waking
is of no use the grasses spread their night across
the series of sounds desperate for meaning and
with quill in hand and atavistic notions about
the spiral and content of the leaf-exchange as
if the epic spawned by such phonetic anguish
it will be certain and red-lined and full of truth
cloud ornament of every vowel and seclusion of
the consonants that don't count the realized
solar homophone at midnight bedlam and hiatus
what a deceit the self of me ! have I ever done ?

the finishing touch is non-duality the margins
where space runs out of time the sense copied
from a dime-novel that language is a dead-end
context of hieroglyph and wedge the Siren-song
the poem I can never start but always finish
on the condition that I'll quite writing tomorrow

07-15-21

A POET'S CAREER

quiet does not suit but loud with wounds
and abscess of time-charged grief a poet
could be living relic of Virgil's heights
or marble chiseled to the bone of some
unknown Hellene living in hieroglyphic
Pharaoh-land a pyramid a caryatid carved
on the top of a broken column a temple wight
a scribbler among the insect tribes who puzzle
with all six feet the meaning of posterity
a poet would be learning that dust is
what remains of sound and gold the assonance
that weights the crown the stuff of legend
and childish myth a library of lost poetry
would be a semblance of some missing vowel
or a Latin lesson's blackboard slate
racing to delete the last word of every line
to make incomplete the excelsior of thought
such a poet not chaste with verbiage
but riddled with the mysteries of breath
whose mind-set is sorrowing at birth
the deathless chasm that lies between sun
and moon Chinese artifact of tone the lees
and dregs of human drunkenness the secret
lover in alcoves and mirrors the adept
of the unwritten word sarcophagus and
bas-relief of the running consonant
velvet-edged infinity opium-perfumed skin
on the chase with idle horses of the Sun

whose waxen hooves have turned to honey
he drops like a planet doomed to silence
into the darkened pool of oblivion AOI
is it not all solitude and darkness ?
no son of Homer nor anyone at all the poet
complaint of a painted Venus dying on the shore
age has shorn and time its scythe
has mown inspirations like ripe harvests
and syntax and language and distance
retroflex noise resounding in shifts and
repercussions of leaf and tide *then* silence
left to dissolve in the summer heat
the dim echoes and hues of memory

07-16-21

AT BREAK OF DAY

in the orthographic wars between the gods
which sound came first which noise was preeminent
to what mortals were given the consonants without
alphabet and what order was assigned to hissing and buzzing
in the great Bang of the origins which syllables defined
destiny and death and why do the children go around
emaciated from silence and the worlds heave into view
with cliffs of repercussion and resonance and the oceans
from which we derive our essence and hearing what
was their role in destroying the established sets of tones
an accent ! a glyph of wind! the trees susurrating nightly
secrets of emphasis and decay and the grasses that lie
down darkening in the repetition of time-past and what !
we wake and divide our selves between aleph and zed
and count from beta to kappa without thinking of
the consequences of a mistaken vowel the fluid and solid
inconstancies of phonetic error speech acts that belong
to statues become ordinary by noon among poets addicts
and seers and before crossing the line that separates hemispheres
of light and derangement consult oracular keyboards
switch from on to off and proceed with caution to the next

lexicon the one arranged by retroflex sounds but in the end
what does it matter whether words have origins or not
or that etymologies cannot go back to the generations
of demi-gods and simply put life itself is in a perplexity
of syntax and matter and the circumstances of sleep-walking
the confusion of ego-perpetuity and amnesia the belt
tied tightly around the temples the issues about divorce
and satiation who can say what meter to emit and how
to restrain the tongue before declaring war and havoc
and the problems of versification of oration and augury
the ability to see past the nimbus clouds of salvation
into the higher promontories of babble and simplification
put to bed the varieties of diphthong and noun-declensions
pastorals of harmony among the breezes and heat-spells
leaves ! talk among them is homogenous and profound
if only humans could learn to listen rather than to go on
walking like corpses in search of a perfect effigy
stammering and stuttering in dreams the interpretation
of hands and automatic writing and divine syllabaries
a wonder that shorelines recede and mountains fly !
the ear is a concussion of history and rumor
and who can ever admit to the primacy of insects ?
is the sun only a homophone blackening by mid-day ?
and life ! the death after death in the stream of consciousness
that begins in astral projections and ends in aphasia
the gods ! orthographic semblances of thunder and lightning
alternatives to language and meaning nothing more

07-17-21

DE SENECTUTE

elephants clouds peacocks—what more do you want ?
old age has set in the great imperishable Autumns !
what more is there to learn but the timeless grammars
and phonetic disruptions of a lifetime grieving
and the required memory of language and tomb
the dumbfounded re-entries into galactic cycles
the primary and secondary invocations to the Muse
and to look out pre-dawn windows at the fading
celestial bodies punctuated by distant rains
dust-storms immolations of water forced denials
of time and its excesses the hardened routines that
obsess then fail at achieving anything but longing
whoever they were the budding nymphs with chalices
and ovations only to bring on dying and repercussion
what is left to surrender but the thin membrane
that bears the imprint of the ever unfinished text
intaglios and ruptured vowels the tarnished onset
of the skies burnish and rub of unspoken margins
failure to admit failure in the due course of things
how green turns to rust and porphyry to sediment
the bottoms of rivers running dry and hides left
hanging on frayed ropes black antelope spotted deer
early winter howling of ancestral animals wandering
lost in the lunar verbiage of permafrost and detour
trying to recall a diner on the turnpike or the small
clump of huts clinging to the afternoon wheel-ruts
and who the people were elders or already dead
who misguided and kept pointing to a missing north
compass of existence ! faces flashing out of speeding
automobiles enormous laughing eternally young
and gone ! the eruption of a volcano round the bend
everyone buried in the mulch of excitement and
upside down tires still turning and the roar of
a proximate heaven the seven trees and their hills
a dialect of aspersion and collapse and bedside
the yellowing tom-toms of echo the faintest hiatus
looking for the painted rocks marking the driveway
apotheosis of the inexplicable consonant of sleep
to learn to lay the head down without expectation

of yet another day in the famous round of hours
elephants clouds peacocks—what more do you want ?

07-18-21

AGELESS MIND

watch nymphs rise from the waters and dry their
hair on floral wharves and follow them as they set
snares for mortals enticing as death the beautiful
garlands and nosegays bouquets of sunburst blossoms
hale and wealthy promises offered in their darting
glances covetous of human error and foiled obsession
them the mind sews in its inner sanctum and pursues
like shadows between the covers of a book of thoughts
all days and weeks all eras of time are but *one* yesterday
the fall from a wagon or a cloud the scraped knee or the bullet
that ends some poor wight's play the designs of vast temples
operatic overtures penny whistles oaten flutes a song
of simple May and hands that tune the keys of melody
or siphon honey from a hive the plans to build a causeway
to cross the galactic seas or to bring swift conclusions
to bankrupt nation states the immensity of language
with all its copied sentiments the raveled and unraveled
texts of sound and pointless noise the structures of air
and the baseless origins of gravity the imitations and
repetitions of memory and longing the speech of leaves
darkening in timeless night the foils and predicaments
of adolescent lovers who turn to witless statues when
noon becomes the acme of a second eternity and the sun itself
spirals of black homophones flaring lamps plunging
with their planetary sisters into the seething void
the ear and eye ! mind's ceaseless spies in the endeavor
to make infinite the spark of birth to render boundless
all the sequences of geology and evolution the very breath
imbued through some magic ornament and mantras
and religious exercises that bring the lunar phases
into the grasp of number and the steps of up and down
the isosceles triangle and the impossible puzzle of dying

mind overloads sweeps under the carpet folds the walls
spreads its eternal childhood out on the front lawn
watching the nymphs bring their partners to the dance
one summer night lit only by the hoards of fireflies
what can the mind know of the body's destitution
missteps phonetic decay disoriented careers aphasia
and worst of all amnesia and oblivion when mind becomes
a dot a broken asterisk a senseless unit in the big enigma
and the nymphs wet and distant grieving so many losses
slowly sink back into the waters that existed before *mind*

07-19-21

LOSING BALANCE

first it was the sidewalk
then the tree beside the sidewalk
the shade it lent to us playing
phantom egos cops and robbers
mappa mundi pirate and traveler
skipping rope with fireflies
guessing blindfolded who or why
evenings forgetting to pray
mumbling sounds instead of words
looked into each other's eyes
the gaze eternal the timeless
instant when we lost balance
each a hand that nothing holds
precarious footing on the cliff
something distant outside of space
nine houses circling a spectral lamp
gravity and the loss of memory
when did it and for how long
the car-ride to a place of death
the swings and corollaries of night
asleep or not the Mexican dialect
the mountain behind the garage
the painted rocks and fallen plums
looking for flying saucers

listening for a dead uncle's flight
into an imagined lunar sea
the comes and goes of reverie
which was you which was me
to this day it's hard to know
the same striped shirt in fade
the same over-size belt dangling
pants and caps and chewing-gum
walking without knowing where
or just swimming all summer long
dog and bicycles and nearby streams
the empty aching sense this was
never the first or second time
but our repeated selves in motion
our speech and silence identical
we stared into each other's eyes
playing charades with strangers
the unknown always *known* to us
a secret from birth to death
but somewhere along the way
unfolding the creased map of breath
you lost your balance , Joe
or was it I who fell by the side
the music we said would play
if one of us were to die
a signal from ancient Tenochtitlan
a flower floating in Xochimilco
a memory of something we never did
the abyss that was always there
opened wide and took first you
and then me into some unrecalled
moment locked in each other's eyes

07-19-21

THE CHINESE SCROLL

for Sarah Cahill

with a flick of the wrist we are atomized
a spectacle of riddled memories and dappled
afternoons of purloined love the landscapes and
waterfalls that misted in *her* eyes and music
of clover and eglantine and volumes unopened
of verses immemorial of times and spaces that
never were and ears drilled with the faint noise
of motor vehicles or machines that fly defying
all odds to meet the gods entranced with their own
soporific majesty spilling ambrosia on Cupid's lap
or simply deaf to the world's entreaties a scene
painted on a single blade of grass a covetous moment
in the dallying of Venus and Adonis or the wishful
deaths of heroes bereaved of the glorious Nymphs
and by one especially flame-haired the daughter
perhaps of emerald and mountain spring the music
of keys of glass and the moon-bright spray of seas
out of arm's reach where bodies fueled by urgency
fulfilled the destiny of souls paired in their foliage
hours cancelled by hours of twilit reverie the roaming
head the mind of chasm and repercussion the reading
of mirror texts of angels burnt by the occasional solar
vowel like ravished copies of Helen or the multiple
effigies of caryatids mounted on columns of great despair
stone and ice the links to an archaic future and abrupt
and loud the parting moment the revealed mattress
the divine disdain for human nerve and ornament
a cluster of cities like tiny gems leftover on *her* cheek
the envelope of empty sonatas promised to be heard
in celebration of the Mausoleum on Asia's other shore
too much ! the number of times the year has come
and gone the varieties of week and month the recall
of calendars the very error and rumor of mortality
windows that open on distant mountain slopes that
seem to vanish in the mists of a dusky Chinese scroll
the deer that chase their shadows and the leaves

07-20-21

THE SPHINX

why are the shades of men by the gods betrayed ?
a summer's afternoon in pools wide and deep
still swim the phantom lads the boys who dived
with glee into the mythic depths ensnared by
love's distant red-haired maiden the Nymph
who preys on death and sweetness all metaphor
archaic sleep in caves with dreams like mountains
charged with blue lightning bolts and streams
that rush through time carrying souls and clouds
far into the cycle of *no-return* fading copies
of memories swift yet vague of days on end when
repercussion and image played havoc in the glass
and words muffled as echoes of unformed sounds
rang the airwaves and radios listened and ears
displayed an ignorance of language and noise
vowel pitted against vowel in the fierce debate
to define the ends but not the means of living
and breath and hot distemper of the guardians
of the Gate and all the while ego-smitten mortals
dress and undress the stories that deceive with
their own mask and stage-craft and grieving
unable to replace pieces of the broken puzzle
rumor is in the winds that shake the famous leaves
poets unknown as the inspiration that breathes within
alone reckon the width and length of the secret hour
it is the woman who started the war piling rock on rock
driving into the wizard night creaking wains and asterisks
stars that inscribe human destinies and planets that
plunge into seething southern seas the very moons
that orbit mind's paltry midnight thought and
light itself that once gone leaves no hieroglyph to
trace with a cautious finger lost in the darkened grass
a lawn ! a fable of might and wrong ! a threnody !
go ask who was the first to write and then erase
the all but unremembered mystery of being

07-21-21

26

TO LIVE OR DIE

such as one who guided me from the cup
of desires where I held my lips to dream
yet fell like a shower of stars into the Sicilian sea
resounding rocks echo of the voyager who
no longer recognizes his homeland adrift fogs
and mists the clouds where souls are lifted
before ensuing the hazards of Purgatorio
am I then one of the dead circling imperfection
of rumor and the multiple errors of love fain
would this be the next world nor the doorways
that seize air and mingle hue and noise with the body
afar I espy the One and am felled by inconstancy
the gaze that turns to stone music of the seven scales
a reading of the mind's proportions of memory
then am enclosed in the suburbs of light and speak
with energy to my double using glass and techniques
of ignition and aphasia to be understood climbing
in the hierarchy of smoke and sound up to the step
that clings to adversity where I remain dumbfounded
in the *first* language when all else is a curtain dropping
and the revelations of rebirths intaglios of distance
the hills where small effigies blind and wriggling
lapse into coma or trance the enormous Voice
that proceeds from the hieroglyph that stands for
Serpent and the rushing and tumult of the moment
each noise is a city of brass and plumes that vanish
a braid of sculpted air a frieze of ether a bas-relief
showing the progress of the knee ! to live or die
the sum of the dice the pegged network of lies
histories of Troy tenfold with at least thirty Helens
composed of sand and combs with no distinctions
but for the homophone of the blackened sun
rising mysteriously on the painted shield of Achilles
it is here I stand and ponder the dim green asterisks
secrets of the zodiac beast and foliage and loss
sky comprised of vowels and punctuated silences
and as ever the eternal unremembered *instant*
--repetitions confusions vacillation

07-22-21

MEDEA : AN APOCALYPSE

"mens immota manet et caeco carpitur igni"
Osidio Geta, Medea

mind remains immobile seized by a blind flame
uttered backwards rivers at a standstill in mirrors
that repeat themselves in silver smoke and
great retributions of history immolations and
bric-a-brac syntax incomprehensible as sleep
the downward plunge and leaden artifacts
exposed one by one and beta particles the riot
and noise of a century dedicated to discrepancies
the atom bomb and the flux of unholy speech acts
swift as carnage in flight or thoughts towed away
by barges of the dead suffused with melancholy
a poetry of rags gathered from the masterpieces
hand-picked by eyeless bards dreams and sulfur
the mega-cities of cloud and ether shimmering
no one can read what it says in mercurial subscript
the iota and delusion of the human wayfarer
standing at the junction trying to recall what
the sphinx said at the midnight repast and Latin
grief and solemnities of grammar and rhetoric
toga and betrayal of the state and hammers
at the door where the enraged hero knocks
prepared to war even with gods the eternal
addicts of sound and lust wanton disregard for
and then the prize held loud and inches away
the armor rusts the tents torn apart flutter
the back door has lost its screen the insects
claim for their own the downcast slopes of Aetna
the classical world is caught in a traffic of horse
elephant and locust while fields burn asphodel
crops breadbaskets overturned and cinders
the folly of statecraft empire of linen and aphasia
each statue each caryatid each solar homophone
soon the semaphores will change and Caracalla
played by a thirteen year old girl named Beatrice
the fusion of technique and *skin* hues and envelopes
hair and hills and the dun-colored dialects alone
she will be reciting lines from a stolen drama

Medea thrill and tragedy in her opium dying
a single hair or a blade of grass is everything

07-22-21

A LOVE LETTER

in the raveled skein of memory ten years is a day
you were in the sense of obfuscation a vacant
issue of the Furies a shower of ancient stars
that ignited your hair the crimson vertigo of
a lost twilight the hills ablaze with torrent
of the solar homophone the black irreverence
of mercy and grace on a platter silver-lined
rim of Sanskrit phonology a bric-a-brac jargon
loosed on the sleeping world transfigured somehow
by the photograph of your smile the iridescent
artifact was a museum you employed to play
music shoulder and fugal structure of a late piece
attributed to the eighteenth century when French
was the dialect of purpose and even today powders
of sulfate and uranium do nothing to disfigure
these aspersions and the great repercussion is that
you still radiate like a planet that cannot darken
despite its plunge into the roiling torment of noon
when seas are most liable to fracture so you may
ask what is this penned fragment this schism of
illumination on the borders of known space
an autopsy of light and leaf the talking left to
philologists ruminating on the void and will
not determine what literature is nor what means
inspiration the wild antecedent to oblivion and
choose as you may the verse will self-destruct
the famous lines the intaglios and cameos *the*
absolutely roseate shimmer of dew as it vanishes
like your skin hypothesis of the next life though
no proof exists of where breath goes the penultimate
syllable in a long ledger of cancellations vague
with premonition and statuary and can I declare

that love is the more *of* less in the unwinding volume
a palimpsest of unpunctuated cloud-physics gorgeous
as are the sunsets reflected behind your eyelids
not a god but a demon comprised of corrupt vowels
the energy of a single lunation or the tonic accent
circumflex and variety of sigmas sleeping in the ear
better the acid detonation of an abandoned summer
the hyaline solution of sky the rhododendron that
pilots the day's waning hour and I am expelled
dumbfounded illiterate on the shoals of a trance
repetitions are good and the likelihood of sound
in its verbal manifestations would we could understand
and leave meaning to the pornographers of reason
for us it was enough that you learned to drive and
afternoons in the wine-wells of longing and the draft
of an eternally unfinished poem a love-letter
thirty years three days in the anarchy of time

07-23-21

FOOTNOTE TO THE SUMMER OF 1953

to what memory does language and its libraries belong ?
a question refuted by common sense the air swells
with image of leaf and the rush of after-school faces
oaths broken and re-taken the folly and erudition
of a book ! hastening into unmitigated darkness
pages obliterated perhaps by tears perhaps by rain
the sweet advantage of just one more glance and Boom !
the world evaporates like gasoline on asphalt a planet
disguised as a lock of hair or a tortoise comb and slowly
rejuvenating effects of verb conjugations in the most
unknown of tongues languid and impossible afternoons
with a piece of chalk scribbling hieroglyphs of love to a tomb
how does a second turn into eternity ? engraved on the back
of an Etruscan mirror the deformed names of Jove and
Herakles beckon from an anterior universe a hand
a token of sound a legend of running water underground
and the effort to make error straight the line both

above and below mind ! a wonder after so many decades
the street still lingers being *there* and nowhere else
heat with its intense and nostalgic repercussion envelopes
the cold grey stone mansions climbing up the hill toward
an invisible tower of motion and noise where the future
begins its odd zigzag course through a monotony of signals
no one is there to stop sleep from consuming itself and voices
the splash and tonic of youth and distance that hold
the remaining diminished quarter of the cosmos in frail
balance or is it because gravity finally becomes visible a fuse
of grass and ether and softened contours remembrance
of the dance partner in all her frill and discipline perfumed
the relief of breath before extinguishing the last firefly
and when the stranger mysterious as all *others* are returns
from his trip to the cordillera to look for the *quetzal* bird
astonishment ! the lyrics of the song at last make sense
ballet of pyramids and oceans the sobbing silver plane
in pursuit of infinity *memory*

07-23-21

MAX : AN EPITAPH

alone the last time I went and sent
scattering the seed of elimination
a recording of the unheard Note
a sky rent in multiples of three
words that defy orthography and
sounds that accompany birth's
first moment and all the rest but
distant hues and motion a noise
of statue and shadow swiftly run
into the swirling yellow air and leaves
and whispering intaglios in the grass
darkening more quickly than the sun
the puzzle of what the augur said
speaking to deformed rock and
heights barely perceived a nerve
that pulsates with joy or fear

ideas that circle above the head and
ears that plead for a silent thread
sleeping is no more a gift and dust
that clouds the waking eye and
aching always to wonder why
the body fails and mothers cry
alone the next time too I'll be
a mystery that I ever came to be
a silhouette a paragraph of echoes
a hand gone limp and cold
someone's memory of me

07-24-21

THE HYMN TO ARTEMIS

Artemis the Archer her high-robed splendor
distance the full sport of mortal-slaying her
in the undifferentiated dawn I espy and
would tear the pages from my book into
the flames toss and keep to the wooded glen
the trough of delight behold where the dead
sun lies vast and empty a blackening sore on
space and listen quiet the fronds and ferns
where ancient voices strain to be heard a
warning a flare in the bottomless night
murmur of stygian waters just inches away
troops of adolescent phantoms and motors
to ignite the years have no sense the months
in alcohol and riot the supreme effort to
overcome and become as a god an iridescent
asterisk plunging through storm clouds and
the cinema of repercussion whom I see slain
a hundredfold in the blazing fields of corn and
rye long since was the moment of recovery
noise of highway engines streaming east
to the still point by the wild fig tree and heat
the encircling past the visions of erased joy
in monuments of sound the struggle to define

and emphasize the human round of births
and what is but grief allotted to the species
Artemis them hunts in their urban lairs
nights on end spent in recording studios or
taverns of endless flow the jargon of insects
that drill the insane ear and to hold but once
most desired the thing to love whence sorrow
and loss the pivot and scheme to endure but
cannot escape her whizzing dart the puzzling
echo that shudders in the talking leaves a drop
of blood that spoils the afternoon in small
groups of nymph and stag the elements defy
who is the first to fall aside into the ditch
felled by her murderous intent and there
unrecognized but mourned and soon forgotten
such are the tales they tell the same story
over and over the passion and its nocturne
instantaneous thrill the embrace and kiss
song that haunts the brain in its passage from
end to end the lightning of unfinished silence
Artemis to whom this stone altar is dedicated

07-25-21

ĀTMAN, the SELF

> "me quoque fata regunt"
> Ovid, Metamorphosis, IX, 432

breath and its twin *all-of-space* a mystery
that existence can be considered at all a sleeping puzzle
and light that falls like rain through the interstices
of some archaic construct of sound and repercussion
echo of all things ! birth between the rungs
of a smoking ladder and noises of fluted joy
that turn to anguish guessing what is inside
the mask who is and is not and what realms
of stone and perpetuity I am at a loss to say why
and solder mind to its insanity of void a pronoun
turned inside out a mirror fractured into infinities

the self am not *I* but some *other* soul whom I grazed
falling from the seventh heaven to the cyclic hells
of Montezuma and the chthonic deities of Teotihuacan
dust-storm in the hummingbird's eye a fraction of number
uncountable seizures of the asteroid that gyrates
above former planet Pluto the divine syllable of childhood
lawns and motor accidents and devastating sores
discontinuity of memory and grass and
the dark railing that marks the other side of nothing
to fathom whence the echo and whither the distance
a stage-play of alter-egos cherubim and demons
ropes pulling the cosmic parts of the body
from order into the renewed disorder of chaos
where nobody is anybody and the refractions of water
and lunging isotope and asterisk and the script
of palsied and illegible scribbling meant to approximate
the human cry the touchstone and screen
the brain's fireflies luminous for an instant only
I am not the child I remember I am not the remembrance
of the death-bed persona I have no self but the other
whom I can never know *et cetera* the fogs of demand
and exclusion the illustrated rock by the roadside
the crypt of envy the pavement of longing do not
and will not meet the definition of meaning only
a lifetime of unstrung recollections
the shape of sky and the size of gold
either the void before birth or the one after death
the great and endless wheel upside down and
turning from side to side across the Ocean-of-Being
and somewhere in the depths of a Dravidian wood
by a placid pool with blue and red lotus afloat
a silhouette holds forth preaching the error
and the rumor of thought to some spotted deer
who have paused to drink their own reflections

07-26-21

MY FATHER'S PAINTING OF TAXCO

a single shadow cast on the street by nobody
silver mines of memory red-tile roofs slanting
into the impossibility that lies behind the dome
with its imposing and reticent syllable
everything is invisible but for the heat in its
various shapes of window and door-frame
a ghost *burro* hooves of the sun sparks of light
noon more eternal than prayers or rosaries
echoing in a vertigo that has no direction
and loud as whispers in a forgotten Toltec dialect
mercury and adobe and voices shouting out
names from Asturias or Andalucía dead provinces
beyond the sea and images of mangled armor
helmets and bloody pikes piercing sugar *calaveras*
with hearts ripped out from the saga of Conquest
this painting left to hang in mid-air for more
than half a century by spectral hands poised
holding a palette with tints and hues of time
which inform an abrupt architecture meant
to recreate taverns or bodegas where yards
of silk unravel revealing a lunar eclipse
or a screen of fireflies to keep night away
daylight is infinite here a perpetuity of yellows
in a feast of crumbling sandstone and dusk
pronouns of smoke and wrought iron arabesques
and doors eternally shut by secret alphabets
the reigning noise is cloudless noontime silence
a fade of flowers dangling from a second floor railing
utterly ineffable nostalgia and repercussion
the vast emptiness of this somnolent town
archaeology of mysticism floating tombstones
captured on a piece of torn canvas with a signature
elegantly carmine at the bottom *Argüelles*

07-27-21

USED BUDDHISM

"el tango era una de las pocas formas
contemporáneas de la tragedia"
Carlos Fuentes, Cambio de piel

how many sutras! diamond and lotus and
empty-land all relegated to a dusty nook
of the most famous used bookstore in the World
clear and right thinking the dhammapada
unsewn hinayana texts jatakamala in Hindi !
tripitaka in Cambodian or Thai allusion to
the first of eight thousand girls born on
the same day as Buddha Shakyamuni
faded field guides to Lumbini in the Terai
Tibetan and Nepali thumb-nail grammars
mumbo jumbo customers stunned and remote
holding crumbling yellow palm-leaf folios
Sinhalese footnotes under the table chairs
partaking of a ceremony repeated in Japanese
translations a hundred ells long and fatigue
to identify the cities on the back of the hand
the geminated consonants in iota subscript
intelligence and repercussion of no use
this is where the gods who've never been born live
the ear is a crashing mountain cataract
eyes flood with letters legible only to the sun
afternoons confined to a single dark echo
countless dog-eared pamphlets proclaiming
the victory of alcohol and celestial mechanics
adolescent kin of the teakwood Arhats loud
and deviant in bright Hawaiian shirts
on a footstool rests the entire Encyclopedia
backwards sideways illogical representations
of what comes before but never what comes after
and the shuffling of a tarot deck or a toss of the I Ching
the Chinese traveler's notes about the visit to Magadha
to gather rumors about the 16 kingdoms the realms
where elephant and tortoise triumph and to
sacred Banaras to hear the tale of the Rebirth
the nascent sky the albescent shell from which
evolve the punctuations and redresses of the Jains

footless mendicants wrapped in orange dyes
what the mind has to empty ! how can one read so much ?
thumbing through text after text in forbidden tongues
prepared if necessary to go lost in jungles
baited with saliva and crocodiles and the Unholy
unexpurgated editions of the Preaching
leave your money behind ! don't buy any of this !
the moment of irreversible transcendence is Here !
what are numbers in the infinite and incorporeal ?
in a labyrinth of print and fabulous illustrations
the brain commits one error after another
and cannot decide whether Nibbana *is* salvation
is it not alone one comes into breath and
alone that one leaves breath ?
everything remains unwritten !

07-28-21

--*THE SACRED DAY WAS WAXING*

the strange break between sunlight and death
like a white opium slowly spreading over the mind
a moment of silence and birdsong and the punctuation
of twigs or branches snapping and the halcyon idea
of water a tempest of surf and wind breathless syllables
of lyric intensity where the road forks into three ways
to go to eternity but which is the straight and which
are the deviant and coruscations of air half a cosmos
to the east of where the body stands waiting to be defined
a hand is its reference a vibrant and momentary index
pointing to the register of hues that are regarded as distance
an event is a thing to expect a moment before the ending
and hesitant and resonant with what remains of sleep
in the eye where meadows print themselves with deer
and the slow evacuation of time before shades interrupt
the lawn with repercussive echoes as if the brother who
shared the birthright were still there in sound and form
but nothing other than a loose volley of pronouns or
a drum-skin pounding its ear of remote hills and despond

why is the section without vowels revealed too soon and
languid artifacts of drowsy splendor falling slowly from
the designation of heaven or gods in the likeness of
insects or hummingbirds graceful in flight and noise
the minutes have no ending and shouts into the shell
and the furious text however illegible presumes a tragedy
the sudden illness or accident the machine and its ditch
sent spinning wheels and the appeal to a higher Being
to no avail the hour has exhausted its last peninsula
the reprieve all wish for was only a rumor reflected
in a shop window for sale the graces and the epitomes
effigies of human reason and the unfinished statue that
promenades in the middle of the thought of infinity if
that can be understood and the out of place consonants
the myth and its detonation the frail and lonely cry
buried in the mysterious silence of the leaves

07-29-21

IMMOBILITY

what a simple day ! it's a matter of immobility
each leaf engraved in the sky is waiting to be memorized
each blade of grass is alert to a future presentiment
have we been here before ? listen to the raucous
chorus of crickets hidden in yesterday's cornfields
someone lies out there waiting to be uncovered
what a myth of unreason *life* ! we will shift gears
in our private motor and lift to the heavens thoughts
imponderable and wordless which dapple our sleep
dreaming there is another world wrapped in ivy
not far from the hospital that gave us birth and sound
we *have* been here before and not just once but persist
in the vague color and transparency of a cloud-bank
metamorphosis of atmosphere and geometry
that seems motionless despite the menace of its shape
like the thin film of a recollection in chiaroscuro
when the many of us became fewer hiking in the hills
do we expect everything to remain the same despite

the ominous development of the rock formation ?
the end of the street was leveled by heat and longing
hint of lilac in the breeze buzz and hum of distance
childhood and the rope of oblivion that circles
the temples turning everything into a stasis
a trance which is *the* instant of eternity and nothing more
so it says in hieroglyph on the verso of the envelope
and the incremental darkness around the knees and
the shibboleth on the airwaves about transcendence
the repercussion and repetition of memory and number
if we *were* here before the simple day is an effigy of
that time motionless homophone of light and depth
how is it the law of gravity is just a photograph ?
where in the world are we today if one of us is missing ?
hand and eye coordinate to bring the seas to a standstill
I lay my head on the painted stone and listen

07-30-21

THE LIBRARY IS A REVOLUTIONARY ACT

libraries are for yarns
spinning tales long afternoons
doing school work looking for books
where they shouldn't be
a dewey decimal disaster confining
all religions other than Xtianity
to a few fractions of a whole
libraries if you work in them
you find sleep an antidote
restless pilgrims march up the stairs
to feed stone lions with thought
is there a way to Yucatan through the back door ?
a pencil sharpener and a busy but
homeless soul reading the Encyclopedia
from Zed to Aleph because a god
hidden in the New York Times
commanded him and Lo
like Charlton Heston

he'll part the Red Sea his head
flat on the long table in the Reading Room
as if there were any other kind of room
and some kids discover poetry next to botany
and others using flash cards and intuition
realize space has negative curvature
as for me I love libraries
I grew up in the children's Room
kitty corner from the Mayo Clinic
later on I learned to shelve books
and stare for hours at the girls
on the other side of the known world
when I became an adult I even earned
a degree in library science
if you can believe such a discipline exists
and got the job I always wanted
a position in the New York Public Library
where one day I introduced myself
to Ezra Pound and believed
poetry was the revolutionary act
that book learning is supposed
to instigate a false notion to be sure
and later I came West and
became disgruntled as a middle-manager
in a serial cataloging unit
doing things I could never explain
not even to my wife
libraries are an uneven participation
in the political ecumene
incomplete collections and
ivory towers labyrinths
really but not a substitute
for universal wisdom
having but a slanted share
in the Cosmic Picture
libraries are meticulous but
erroneous ways of indexing
everything they can get their hands on
now it is all being digitized
and the ideas that go in loops

on master negative film splices
simply get lost in the aggregate
of details and on-line mechanics
libraries are a way of destroying
the knowable and cancelling
the past with a blind-spot
vision of perpetuating it

07-29-21

PERPETUUM MOBILE

leaves that plagiarize human memory
as we darken on the tip of a peninsula
that extends like a blade of grass into eternity
are we what's left of all we used to know ?
fewer than us and no more than a cipher
that sustains us in a perpetuum mobile
the world is a scum pond of illusion
fretwork of unknown stars and gods
without origins fluted columns of sound
noises and bric-a-brac meaningless syllables
the omicron of envy and the lambda of
divisiveness colored elements and particles
that flutter falling from one dream into another
voices of children who dwell deep within
in their small bird-like Latin almost argent
but soon turned to whispers of rust and loss
one after another felled the playmates
of the drifting continent the apogee of nothing
skies that wander like pollen in an afternoon
that lasts eight decades in a single hour
and to bed but where in this loose labyrinth
of repercussion and soundless echo ?

07-31-21

THE OTHER HALF OF THE POEM

all of this is but half a poem a fraction
of what I need to say but cannot the more
time diminishes its portion of eternity
the less I am able to number the sounds
and echoes of words I cannot remember to say
illusory noises that occur in the sleeping ear
waking figment of the past a landscape
of capsized mountains folded into a bed of grass
or leaves torn from the lexicon of meanings
which is and where are and to whom address
these rambling invocations to a god unknown
the one whose half is vanished in the dust of moths
the craters of the moon and the divisive homophone
of the blackened sun and the stars themselves
green errors wandering syllables in a tempest
of recurring cycles of heat and destruction
the universe ! a Buddhist template of vertigo
kaleidoscope of endless imitations and rebirths
the lists of libraries with their varying diphthongs
the histories without end that are gathered
on the tip of a wobbling toy and the smokes
and ladders and adolescents who copy
our every move in a glass that rotates
with the motion of the traveling mind
and am I this thing in the midst of rumor
who regrets each passing *memento mori*
that I cannot catch and keep hold of what I
cannot possess the loves and bitter playthings
the ends of threads and driven drum-skins
a ploy this world to walk about and seek to
enter but at every turn fail to find the door
and still to traverse nocturnal seas and grief
condemned to never finish the other half
of this witless string of words this poem
with its haunting empty hemispheres
with its longing to remember

07-31-21

42

AS WE WALKED HOME FROM THE
POOL ONE SUMMER AFTERNOON

is what recalls the body the soul itself
a shadow's tale on a summer day a flight
of thought the other life the one that came
before if such a circle persists in time
and heat that devours the southern clime
takes wing abandons weight and flies
the thing slight as dust-mote or feather
cries separating from the lamp its mind
tender trace of being and then no more
can it be it was just a text of fingertips
called memory a repercussion of longing
and sun and leaf travel across
realms of invisibility and oblivion
that punctuate the encircling atmospheres
air and its dualities of light and dark
blow the winds without direction
and tempests in love with tree and rock
like the incoherence of expiring breath
released from its secret shape and sound
the soul ! from afar the nymphs shake
water off their skin and learn to mourn
long hours without a pronoun to address
the famous legends are turned to stone
language is but a dream gone wrong
that words fail to realize and echoes
ravel through clouds a list of names
mortals ! the body is not reborn
nor are mysteries ever revealed
the enigma is the unseen integer
sacred inside the uncounted cipher
there is no back or front nor east
that ever collides with west only copies
of unreason in multiples of personality
masks the *others* wear forgetting not
who they are but that they have ever been
summoned by some unheard noise
we come hesitantly to the edge
haunted by what we cannot recall

and watch as winged beings vanish
into the burnished envelope of time

08-01-21

THE GOVERNMENT OF THE WORLD
para mi hermana Laurita

such as it was the large park with its gentle slope
that covered the eastern hemisphere with a playground
and swings and slides and empty moments of transgression
did we not realize that coming home too late
meant the reversal of the order of moonrise in the bushes
smell of lilac and heady somnolence adrift like insects
who have lost their sense of touch and yes a movie
carried with it the longing to be someone else an *other*
who bore the stigmata of a previous life sleeping
in a flower bed the hour it takes a moth to evolve
we learned to listen for punctuations between planets
and the eerie sound of metal hurtling silently through space
a cardboard castle a realm of sand and gravel surrounded
by rocks painted by father Jupiter a lookout
near the forbidden window where invalids of life
kept to their beds of tobacco and sugared skulls
which of us was the first to know there was no deposit
no famous ruin of money nor sunsets in dialect
the opprobrium of another hemisphere beyond
the casual sentence of oneiric drift seemed ominous
the menace of a day unmarked on any calendar or
the sudden and monstrous dark of the only Catholic Church
near the movie-theater and drugstore and underground walkway
we divided the town in half and the halves in quarters
until the cosmos itself was a microscopic map
with cities and battles and futile names for governance
everything that could ever happen did in a split second
between the opening of the liquor store and the dead automobile
that careened out of control in Uncle Ernie's brain
by turns we each got sick with chills and visions of Mercury
religion was to no avail nor the unfolding of a thought

books and their likenesses the hills and highways
that offered pyramids and intellect of photographic distance
we learned nothing by tarrying on porches playing charades
with the girls who were born with automatic memory
how could we know that futures of disaster and presentiment
were in their perfumed embrace the dance of infinity
fire-flies and the remote thrill of those stained lips
if we could have remained untransformed rather than isotopes
verging and diverging on a dizzy spiral into a universe
that was emerging from a second inception of time
the government of the world ! it was in the design of our hands
on the large papers we spread out on the deep green rug
the radio in either ear the sockets that we plugged in
to speculate on our previous existences to prove there
were others to come in the divinity of inspiration
****

this is an autobiography never to be completed of a dead twin
irreversible recollections of a time and space when
both were an indissoluble pronoun that cannot be discerned
the half of light and the half of darkness that cannot join
playground and pool the foundation of water and leaf
the integument of night as it encircles the secret language
the very brief and terribly fragile moment when neither one
could ever be separated from the other come a lifetime
of grief and enigmatic prophecy--
pyramids of the Sun and Moon !

08-02-21

THE END HAS COME AND GONE

in the hot south of France where history conforms
to routes of dust and infinite heat and still the din
that hovers over Carcassonne's near perfect battlements
and the riot and glint of metal and catastrophe
infusion of heresy and distilled Romance dialect
the singing and gorgeous plague of love and parity
all this and more the instant comes to bear on hues
more yellow than daffodil or dandelion a burning

that ravels the air into fists of angry melody and
whatever cannot be discerned in the sun's blackening
passage across the tumult of a destroyed landscape
but these are all just twisted asides footnotes to a
greater sum of nothingness tawdry and renowned
biographies and litanies mortals litigate erecting
stiff wind-defying banners and color the eons of air
blood stained and puce and furs and stoles that adorn
shoulders of well designed women whose promenades
across a paper stage intensify the heraldry of smoke
fogs and spells that litter school books with lies
furtive illustrated grammar drills that proclaim
one nation state's grievance against another in wars
that take centuries to enervate the academic brain
revolutions and genealogies of domination by surprise
and what ends in great disregard in threnodies or odes
false strips of parchment called literature and skies
that blister in arcane deliveries of pronoun and
registries of give and take the ominous census of
asterisks in quantity and the hovels and chattel of
servitude ogres of human progress machines and oils
and metal wings that fly and atmospheres like ringing
ears that madden diplomatic cables with conspiracy
how much to learn and unlearn Gaul divided by three
and the rivers and mountains and haunted woods
where emperors staked victories by a throw of dice
in what world can this happen ? is Japan any better ?
do the many hued miniatures of Mogul dynasties
outdo the glitter and powdered wigs of Versailles ?
a Buddha comes from the fabled east to preach
unknown on the curbsides of Rue Mouffetard
the end has come and gone the chronicles lack sense
the written word like its echo the forged syllabary
has been dissolved in inks and pastiche of the gods
envious of the mortal debacle of broken trust
forsaken are the laws of reincarnation the karma
and dividends of dharma that naked seers in ovens
used to recite in the Vedic enterprise of thought
vanities all the north and south and metaphysics of cloud
saffron robes up in flames distances brought to naught

underfoot the roiling seas and temptations of loss
that bear no fruit and longing for a different birth
Buddha holds forth to silences of stone and tree
his inner eye his monocle of dispatch and isolation
the wearied tread of minds that have lost the way
he discerns and says no more than a statue might
deluded by the brightness of this eternal noon

08-02-21

THE ORIGINS OF VALUM VOTAN

you were no more immortal than a blade of grass
it was eternity you sensed when the heat doubled back
taking with it lawns and purposes and fallen leaves
as you pushed the mower back and forth over a strip
of yard that resembled a dark subcontinent and
listened carefully for the chorus of insects brooding
in the tiny Himalaya of gravel and pulled weeds
great was the moment when the gods shimmering
in their Sunday best leaped from the rooftops
you saw them ! the minute passed a sound of wings
scouring invisible realms of azure and porphyry
seemed to zoom and buzz with the alphabets of bees
or the blurred ecstasy of the hummingbird's asterisk
flight was possible the path to immortality and memory
what was to do but levitate into the sack of night
you began to count the number of times darkness
recurred in geography books and the unconscious
a letter at a time and soon the entire cosmography
of the ninth grade was spelled out in red brick dust
no one heard you and you heard no one in a trance
the size of an ice-cube draining the air of colors
the epitome of all religions scribbled on the sidewalk
in orange and yellow chalk the secret of the universe
in the awkward rectangles where you jumped on
one foot only imitating the Vedic rishis blind drunk
in either hand potions drugs booze soma magic elixirs
in didn't matter the language you spoke lacked grammar

vowels and diphthongs and the mastery of consonants
the next minute which occupied the other half of time
was when you came out of *it* picking your head up
from the concrete where you had fallen from the wagon
and everything was red and curtained in drapes
of vibrating ether and the noise of aerial motors
carrying the enigma back to its celestial text
you were caught in the revolving door of infinity
immortal ! but for a brief instant only and then
you were sweating pushing the lawnmower again
as your father had ordained over a copy of earth
the sun bearing down on you its black homophone
& you began slowly to unravel the fiction of being
thunder clouds and a gust of indigo wind
everywhere the back and forth before birth !

08-03-21

ANCIENT LANKA FOUND ON NO MAP

strings of neuter nouns flowers in profusion
growing on trees with exotic names and cities !
the shape of women with balconies like earrings
and creatures that capture shadows and eat them
pools and ponds and undergrowth lush and red
and orange and the chattering ear and the sleeping
mouth and the eye filled with seven versions of sky
Lanka ! set in the middle of the southern sea
all the ways to and from the citadel of Death
and a language constructed of oral batteries and
vowels that have no sound and climbing up and
down the peaks that scrape heaven's distant girth
secret panoplies and awnings stretched across
the illusion of a moving earth and files and rows
of armed warriors with bodies like green pods
and arms the length of evening bearing weapons
glistening gold and minerals dug out of whispers
clay and potters' wheels and brilliant shining pastes
a story of ships that climb and portals to the other side

and bearing news of lotus-feet and Renunciation
and snakes and elephants and tortoises on whom
the universe rests as it readies for the birth of time
no language can exhaust the scripts evolving from
palm leaf or banana stalk and prodigious words
that have no meaning and echo rutilating through
a dream of asterisks and retroflex oracles
how many the minute insect kings whose battles
consume volumes of ancient epic collusions and
flame and altars and staggered temples colossal
with sculpture of a million eons now long past
the gone and the whirlwind and the phases of
a lunar mystery the umbilical season of space
haunting crevices where rain is born and clouds
magnificent as arches of lightning a hundred-fold
the movie theater where Brahmans doze and
waking envelopes of crimson powders and hands
that catch winged souls that try to flee mortality
this all in an instant of nascent light and *Boom !*
the conflagration that has no beginning and
yet finds us walking in a trance of ambulances
and sirens grieving the loss of memory children
whose eventualities are error and repercussion
rumor that this may not be the first of the many
lives in a string of celestial detonations and pause
laying the head on its archaic stone to listen
to what has never been foretold and to sleep
the darkness that wraps the knees and disappears

08-04-21

DEFINING MIND AND MATTER

the voice on the phone burst out crying
upon hearing the unbearable news summer
would never return again and light and
the varieties of sound and the mystery
of cloud formations that disappear when
the eye turns to sand and sleep the concussion

of direction wayward systems of heat slight
implosions in the nerve that leads to the brain
a day can only last so long before forever
takes hold and angels with stolen wings
that hover on the ledge three inches above
the thermometer like statues of glass and purity
witnesses to the failure of noon to keep
its equestrian satellites ablaze in the sun
whose rotating thumbs darken the hours
blotting out windows of childhood stanzas
wasn't supposed to come so soon the call
the infinite silence that abandons longing
to the last letter of the alphabet
breathed into a hemisphere of cold ether
far from the island of misused consonants
and hills of mourning and lawns tilting
into the unforgiving sea of vision poetry
the rest they call a strike-out a field
of noisome worries a plethora shouting
to get past the skin to the inner valves
where the self destroys itself inchoate as
a smokeless flame on the altar of desire
and left to ponder how much more
to grieve the ineffable side-stepping clause
to give to the gods what is not theirs
to receive in return the errors of mind
we live on rumor assumptions of love
as if it were matter imperishable somehow
levels of ego and personality and shadows
the effigies we embrace sleeping adrift
only to wake startled required to imagine
an inconstant series of passing images
copies of distant memories talking
in echoes and vanishing in crematoria

08-05-21

LOVE'S TIMELESS WOUND

"et nihil est annis velocius"
Ovid, Metamorphosis, X, 520

for indeed the race of lions I detest
and the tusked wild boar whose eyes
blood-thirsty ring terror in a thrill
to prolong risk and danger spoke
Venus to her boy-love addled Adonis
on shores of poetry and lissome meter
as brisk breezes through leaves recited
elegant hexameters and loud in shells
the sea's violated testimonies and from
above celestial bane and indifference
but careless of words and warning
the adolescent sure of his own glory
with alcohol racing in his heart to
magnify the luster of his locks while
speeding on his own two-wheeled
emotion skimmed past the laws of
nature into shoals beyond sunset
stars a-glimmer in the forever past
as all things are dead before they're
born and the repetitions in glass and
mercury that lend repercussion to
effigies of sentient beings be they
enamored of their own souls or of
the ones they most resemble and
like flowers on a river bank by noon
are turned to dust and the shrill
reeds that ply the ear with sounds
of distance and memory disappear
leaving rust and lunar decay in
the cracked vault of the gods
whom none implore being forsaken
bereft Adonis heedless of the hunt
nor can added years perfect his image
victim of illusion's longing syllables
as sweet death's bee-swarms drain
the atmosphere of all sound he now
succumbs to love's timeless wound

for one brief second ampersands
that separate light from the world flare
like planets plunging from their cars
invisible wings the roar of unshaped time
velocities of matter and gravity
the soul's unseen hieroglyphs
darkening in the shapes of leaves

08-06-21

HIROSHIMA : SHADOWS OF MEMORY

still another anniversary of that reckless day
concrete blistered like frail plum blossoms
shadows of men pasted to earth's surface
silent cries that fill the fatal mushroom cloud
how indistinct the mind of presidents and emperors
shuttle-cocks and winged monsters puzzle
the oriental skies with energies and oracles
with hierophantic and instantaneous instructions
to deliver the world of its bad karma
and shatter forever the peace of the eons
planets come and go in the Buddha's sleeping ear
stone and rock the illusion of heaven's heights
trees that run burning with enigmatic punctuations
the atom ! at play with Nature's indiscretions
split divide multiply subtract and annihilate
numbers and the congress of zeroes hyphenations
and hiatus the poetry of a million suns
the blaze foretold by Krishna and Arjuna's chariot
hurtling through the fifty hemispheres of space
what monstrous vowel the unexpected *Boom !*
transfigured deserts seas that have no bottom
the beginning that comes after the end
galaxies pivot like grains of blazing sand
on the painted screen of oblivion
repercussions ! the unborn gods asleep
in the reincarnation of memory

08-06-21

52

TODAY'S WEATHER REPORT

the world bubble palaces constructed of precious
gemstones gardens where peacock and elephant
roam free and winds bearing nets of folly and destruction
the emperor on the left of the photo extinguishing light
and the dukes and earls and petty magnates at his feet
and skyscrapers aroused from sandpaper and saliva
everything lasts less than a minute before new planets
are discovered on a microscope lens and the insects
whose chisel-like intelligence removes water from
water and what else is there in this passing stanza
to believe that somehow we can escape mortality
and address envelopes with gilt letter-head and seek
to fly the very next day with new bought wings of wax
and silken thread ornaments of love ! juxtapositions
of state and county and the thrill of hunting at three
in the morning before the airports open their tents
we too go wandering the fabulous parks of memory
chasing gauzy things that flit in the mental air and call
out names to each other with assumptions of ego and bliss
it is waking on a stage with great props of cloud and thunder
lightning streaks the western screens and hills come and go
do you really think we can get out unscathed ? a chill
watching rare species die within minutes of the rain
and sections of atmosphere are cleaved from the error
of outer space and we continue to shout in sleep for
some sort of transport that offers salvation and an extra
day should this one end too soon and the engines of
revival and alimony sit idling outside the mansions
where demons strut like fancy gods in nylon hose and
turbans wrapped tight around their fictitious heads
it is like a movie theater one late afternoon in Chicago
and outside the heat packs its saddle-bags and mounts
war against human progress and we exit the arena
and consult our histories to discover it is the day after
time and nothing we have accomplished bears fruit
we lean against balustrades with murals depicting
the evolution of the soul from trilobite to mysterium
and wonder the places we have been are no more and
a single asterisk lighting the southern hemisphere

sparkles on and off its meaningless display of sky
what have learned ?

08-07-21

FLY ME TO THE MOON

fifteen years since we parted , Bro'
really but only three hours since your plane
lifted off for the fatal southern hemisphere
you took the front yard with you and the willow
trees by the side with their sacred branches
and the painting on the bedroom wall azure
sea with its single tropical island and the bunk
beds and lawn-mower and the gravel and
painted rocks I've said it all before depth
has no dimension and width is an illusion
don't understand the terrain things lifting
up into the air a voice without sound comes
up to my ear whispering zetas and humming
could just be the paper boy the shy diffident
reading Camus and Gide before his time and
gravity is a lesson in twelfth grade and just
when we learned to drink and overdo it
the guy in the rearview mirror will guide us
to the turnpike on our way but separately
to Manhattan a thumb and an elixir of joy
burst of poppies brighter than what's in
the eye Turkish drams of coffee broken arm
on some Greek rock you'd write back half
the tome was an anniversary of the cigarette
the other illegible library of incidence and
repercussion vowels and sideways glances
at the girl with the top-knot wasn't her name
but never mind from Kansas and the doctors'
daughters all full of French art vying for
you even as the plane entered forbidden
plots of atmosphere Mayan tanks flooded
with blue and red lotus the spire and stalk

jotting down botanical references for peyote
drawers of infinity the gas leaking from
the upper story where the brain's etymology
you looked back at me looking back at you

08-07-21

HYDE PARK BLUES *ca. 1960*

they said a jump start would do it
no money in the bank some trust
in the obvious deities and friends
a vision to peddle wasteland and
overtime in the night-ward of bedlam
situated some north of the degree
lunar phases set aside for push to
marijuana beds and face-down
in lotus mire the plots sickened
who would know whatever comes
that may be all that happened
flash of bright some ammonium
a rigged sound of pyramids climb
and dust the paper flowers and bees
slung together on lysergic acid
suddenly it's Paris and Bohemia
unknown to the self a quandary
in letters and art graduated fifth
with a flask in hand the surgeon
general said it was a nightmare
German rucksacks packed with
palimpsests and art history theory
of the *Modern* abscess and splint
transformative forays into future
backdrop of Miles Davis be-bop
birth of the cool second to none
Señor Blues barefoot on 63rd street
under the "el" three in the morning
where oh where can my bonny boy be
a song full of reefer or push a button

to erase reflections and slide into
illegal basement clubs so fucking hip
just like the brothers in underwear
doing a Muddy Waters mojo trip
field hollers and incendiary minds
ice-knife winds off Lake Michigan
looking for the keys lips busted open
scram a deal standing there half-frozen
what did I know, Officer ? my hands
was free my brain was elsewhere a
red signal a long ride back and forth
on the Illinois Central hunh *frapp!*

08-08-21

HAPPY BIRTHDAY TO EVERYONE!

holy all the days that have never been
holy all the persons stained by renunciation
frequencies of light intermittent vacancies
the world is no older than its newsprung grass
yet fires and deep chill and aggravated speech-acts
voices from inferno hoarse and excavating
and hail-stones of granite and the burning eye !
holy the soul most active when inert and silent
business partner of the gods transacting bodies
in the market place of transfer and rebirth
holy memory with its dactyls and spondees in reverse
the antiquities of the chopping block the flesh
hung out to dry in the winds of eternity
how much has happened in the two seconds
it takes to clip the wing in mid-flight
and see ! earth tumbles in its dizzy gyre
sport of Nymphs and reckless avatars who descend
the Mountain to destroy their lovely bauble
and of all the gods none can be called *most* holy
Hosannah in the midst of atmospheres
where painted screens and failed motor vehicles
list in the anatomy of history erased by time

holy oblivion of language and invisibility
the indissoluble knot the unheard Note
the myths of infinite recurrence and sight
holy this day if it has ever been
these modules of lamp and effervescence
this sense that the end has no beginning
holy the transgressions by which we name the self
the inflection of a word that cannot be found
the hand that breaks its own wrist and pines
longing for the shoulder's distant height
holy and *holy* again the viscera of mind
lost in its labyrinth of thought and error
rumor of infinity in a sleep that cannot wake
holy the indifference of the world at large
the two thousand Buddhas of anticipation
who dwell in ant heaps and cities and floods
holier still the rock whose birth none has seen
whose death none will ever notice
holy the south haunted by spirits and alcohol
holy the demons great and kind whose clouds of fire
and sulfur and intimacy bring us together
on this day if it has ever been
holy

08-09-21

JACK FOLEY AETAS 81

sitting on a promontory that could be
Howth Head or the rugged Gibraltar peak
or even the more familiar Berkeley Hills
in whatever dialect you say it
however depth you aim to speak
with whatever vocal chords and
vowels simpatico and evanescent
whoever cares to listen to the eaves
where leaves whisper their autumn latest
whichever year it could be in passing
eighty plus one and the temperature's rising

garden-foot sedimental beacon
trouser-flung brain sling
the each of you that compose your mind
the persons of a fellowship of invisibility
the ego of rust the flight of the shoulder
bee-swarm of intellect many-eyed traveler
in music dustbin of antiquities and modernist
with two harp-strings per ear
Sing old maudlin fool ! Orpheus !
'tis your annual coming around
the circle as it widens into infinity

08-09-21

THE GREEN GUITARS

the crescent the fold the enervated deer
confused that wander distance like a park
on the fringes where mountains dissolve sinking
into the mind's insatiable longing for symbols
death is the partaker of this sunset glow which
swallows most of the empyrean in its glance
even thousand-eyed sun trembles blackening
in the wake of some forsaken thought about
the afterlife and why does the patrol that circles
the hour nightly not discern ? a roadside motel
where mortality rents a bed to watch TV all night
'til dawn finds the bracken soul half-crazed
looking for the latch and haunted voices
black and white seem to shred the smoking air
and hands borrowed from the Apostles scour
the walls for secret clues to the spaces between
asterisk and ampersand the stars livid and guttering
how the heavens shake ! scatter the small animals to
their lairs and speak the leaves their nocturnal talk
and falling like meteors out of a hollow planet
angels with soot around the eyes and cauterized
at the joints where wings should be supplicate
the remnants of the gods for a justification for flight

all ends in the saddened lake of light and breath
the losses tabulated in the grass missing fingers
combs and shattered cups the reading of the names
lists of noise and extravagance and the weeping
in the embers the unlit windows the gravel and
the sheets left to dry on the unnumbered rocks
a woman with the moon for a face bearing
the gravity of lotus and ivy in her embrace cries
out for Orpheus for Adonis for Horus cries out
the green guitars make a plangent sound like
clouds coming to rest on the other side of sleep
the green guitars that play until the wind no
longer sees its reflection in the rushing stream
and deer feel the weight of time no more

08-10-21

BIG BANG SUTRA

oh how great is sky the mercury dented
as it circles high the almighty endlessness
of azure beyond control the artifact of thunder
and tinfoil the rattling fluorescent streaks
and thirsty the countless more than three thousand
gods in their photo format best strutting illusory
figures of a past that has ceased being important
what is the objection to infinity ? planets grown puny
wobbling on flickering electric filaments and the joke
about the Big Bang and the retorts and syllogisms
about Black Holes the warmongers' treasure chest
panoply of future lives fodder for religious zeal
unwritten texts about string theory and dialect
continuums across eighty million galaxies
the constant defection of mind and immortality
flowerbeds of myth trolling the airwaves for a voice
a shadow an echo of sound copies of radioactive
noise effigies of invisible entities who govern thinking
radical numbers square root of zero synapse and
delusion of language babble and augury all amounts

to solitude the virtue of introspection in the dilemma
of a star-spent cosmos illiterate and baffling at best
dream forms hallucinations drug addiction before birth !
whatever we squander in love in flights of fancy
in crossing seas of intellect and no-mind
whoever we ourselves might be in this puzzling lack
of syntax in this bedlam of recreation and selfishness
this is not me ! so you declare to the daily mirror
folding the ego like a newspaper and tossing it into the bin
awards and acclamations ! the loosened dust of chimeras
flames that eat retrograde signals to become *other*
when was the child ever more than a mask playing
a satellite of someone else's shadow performing
innocence like a gong before falling into a coma ?
there it is the epic of leaping the ocean to search palaces
mysterious and gorgeous with love-drunk women who
have lost notion of self and gorge themselves on their own
likeness over and over 'til dawn finds them mutated
into zombies of apparel and luxury clothing on glossy pages
of international magazines that feature poetry
as the next big thing all the universe unravels !
Big Bang never happened ! it's a Japanese hoax
an aggravated and repeated repercussion ad infinitum
of an unrepeatable history of the cyclotron and the atom
Buddha in the thousand and ten mirrors of oblivion
preaching loneliness beneath the Bodhi tree
everything is an aspect of illusion the mirage of matter
the ascent and descent of air when a day lasts
a million epochs and an epoch is a butterfly's lifetime
tat tvam asi

08-11-21

PLATEAU EVEN HORIZON PEACE HARMONY NO-MIND

stunned the myriad-eyed god of repercussion and dialect
leans on his crooked staff and roars the silence of eons
galaxies form in a single vowel a noise of refracted suns
elegance of space evolving on a simple thread of light
until the whole turns inside out and planets burst like
daisies the day's eye and sunflowers and the backyard
teems with insects of intellect and see-saws brilliance
of breathing and sleep between punctuations of air
coming to be and going out of consciousness the same thing
always the instant when eternity turns like a crazy top around
a chalk sign and evenings descend with loud but vanishing
children whose names are reflections of water and emptiness
myself the you I think we are together the other One divided
zygote of anima and animus registries of hexameter and zero
we are in the snow at age four and at age nine in a summer
that has at either end a large city drawn and quartered on paper
and before the next century our intelligences exhumed and dusky
all but missing on the x-ray of human activity but resonating
across seas and continents of hue and echo the various world
the pastiche of envy and corollary the bottom of sand and brief
as everything is transitory as ambulances careening urgently
toward a planet yet to be named a hospice and an oasis
that nothing has a truth inherent and cloud and grass are all
we needed to know lying on our backs on the ridge of infinity
before the epos of satellite and divination and hieroglyph
escorted us climbing the instamatic Pyramids of sun and moon
it all happened in a photograph and has not recurred ever since
it is a flicker in the back-mind a passage of lighted windows
that darken no sooner does the thought occur that though
we are coming home we will never get there

08-11-21

SCHOOL DAYS

Soon as three o'clock rolls around
You finally lay your burden down
                    Chuck Berry

I'm still in high-school learning how to *be*
on one side fields of alfalfa and corn summering
on the other a phantom Mary Lou the borrowed
replica of a goddess who never materialized fully
but which is more powerful the god of Rain or
the homophonic and dyslectic god of Fire ?
football players scoff the new home-coming queen
kids stand in the middle of traffic daring to die
everything is ancient before it has come to term
the ever fleeting instant of *never-been* alcohol
the first cigarette growing up to encourage envy
foment spite and to increase arguments like sport
the rah-rah of moonglow and pleated skirts
held by large safety pins a-swirl with asterisks
the most is already over and the bleachers are
packed with Friday-night ghosts and a radio full blast
no one can hear ! night is a distilled amphetamine pill
shortcomings of destiny without definitions and
pullover skin and hoods with a thousand eyes
like serpents from the Bhagava Gita and songs
that emanate from convertible vehicles mad
to traverse the seasons of insect and longing
who is the greatest of Prophets if not *Valum Votan ?*
back-seat romance and tragedy liquor death and
highway patrol squads looming by the bend where
hieroglyph and cuneiform meet to create literature
in its 9th grade version of accident and declension
the riots are in the left ear only the perpetuity
of noise descended from Indo-Aryan ancestors
the mountains of enormous antiquity are but
an illusion in a glass of cherry coke and one
by one the lunar syllables evoke nostalgias
for the origins of sound the wordless centuries
that precede textbooks of biology and French
who can say why wars are still fought because
of Helen and the sophomoric messages of Apollo

puzzled by the movie account with Silvana Mangano
playing both Circe and Penelope the kids decide
to cheer on the Cyclops and fail to understand
that they are already dead beyond redemption
on the outskirts of town where the County Fair
sets up rodeos and stock-car racing grounds
life is an alphabet without a first letter a ruse !
after a few years they all disperse erased singly
and oblivious of their birth pronoun and seized
by the hair by a playwright of monologues
sky-script cloud begotten solemnities grief
the art of forgetting written on autumn leaves

08-12-21

WHEN THE LORD OF NUMBERS
HAS CEASED COUNTING

nothing more left to say
the tide has pulled earth away from its rim
edges fray space shrivels in its own womb
no new day no burst of ornamental light
no sun to drive its blackened steeds
across the opaque library sky
merely the dumb countenance of angels
amazed that mortals have lost sway
the steps that lead backwards into the arena
the lions and cicadas and Chinese astrologers
who toss sticks and make cities out of wet sand
erecting pagodas that scrape the clouds
awnings of smoke blurred sounds in *italics*
hours that are numbered by the leaf
intellect and grammar and nose-bleed
narcolepsy and love-potions *the world* !
such as it is memory strains to recollect
the day before yesterday the moment before birth
essences and perfumes the wafting incense
and ciphers that constitute the archaeology of air
a suitor is at the door demanding Helen back

the poet bruised in the left heel stutters
in desperation to recount the death of Achilles
there is a fifth sea ! pearl-necklaces jade ear-rings
palaces and hovels suburbs of pharmocopeia
the kids are learning to drive their motors
across fields forgotten by the seasons
where insects reign with a multiplied intelligence
the purpose of sidewalks is to sustain emotions
the kids are mad to own the shape of Desire
hands fumble at mismatched keys
there are doors with only one side
and augurs and oracles and islands of porphyry
no one benefits from salvation and number
it is longing and the intensity of lipstick that matter
people rotate masks before five in the afternoon
mirror echoes mirror in the house of Madness
a drill works its way through a maelstrom of silence
noise ! art and the cacophony of mind !
each day is no day at all in outer space
planets gorge themselves on anti-matter
quanta and dialects of mountain twilight
the kids wish they'd never been born !
aching to have an hour of darkness without minutes
listening for the soundless Note in havoc
delivery from Temptation ! sometimes it is only
the wounded glass with its geminated shoulders
the wrist and the forfeit and the mortgage
so little is known about immortality !
infinity is one less than nothing !

08-13-21

EST SPECUS IN MEDIO
Ovid

the poets live on a thread of light
name changes speculation of unreason
there are so many words for *One* !
yet they bicker and babble about the Many

the single and the complex the *hapax* and
the phenomenon of mind labyrinthine
and totally multiple an egress to pastoral
and eclogue and bucolic and elegy
hexameters unraveled on a salty wave
sailors beware ! red waters of the depths
insanity is at the root and the gorgeous
voice of the bacchants at dawn seesawing
the air with loss of cognition and aphasia
it is for this the poets are in love with Love
faulty flawed decaying in the middle vowel
absorbed and absolved of intellect like insects
devouring the medulla of heat accompanied
by the noise of their wings the flight of nerve
and the sutures in glass and the opaque
memory of the life before this one
a hazard of hues and distances without sound
cipher after cipher of resonance and repetition
victims of ecstasy and desire and grief
to be reborn ! to generate thumb and tombstone
by the roadside waiting for the oracle and the tree
blossoms that will never wilt days without night
relating on the one hand the overture to time
and on the other ignorance and bafflement
the poets unable to recognize one another
Ovid Ariosto Góngora Lorca and Lamantia !
there is a mirror in the middle
it is an unknown canto of Dante loud
and specious with the epiphany of consonants
radiating from the Rose of immortality
seconds pass and everything goes numb
fertility of dust ! pronunciations without lips !
tomorrow it will go back to the year 1956
the sun will come into being black and awful
adolescent lies about Greece and India
Spain with its green guitars and France !
sightless the renewed poets will start
making claims of originality and longing
there will be bookstores of discovery
and headless rock formations that sing !

08-13-21

THE ORIGIN OF LITERATURE

the voices of light still audible
the bright passage from one dark
to the other in the firmament of mind
stellar abductions of body and soul
redactions of a wholly imaginary text
the living fundament time after time
invoked as fragments of memory
written in dust or mown grass fading
in the hills where shadows go with
recollections of what was once solid
and stirring in a movement of leaves
how far the sound travels into seas
found only on library shelves the remote
and sorrowful monuments of antiquity
give no pleasure distraught images
Troy was here and the burning and
sobbing and the shore came up to this
street and the boats hauled and caulked
ropes and battered sails the winds
unraveling colors into a faded diorama
sand and canvas and insect hovels
the itching and strain of language
meter and pitch accent and fraught
with error and clouds booming black
and ravenous over the eclipsed town
and shivered landscape corn fields
devastated by hail and tiny flags like
hands mourning the gone earth
the kids puzzling over declension and
intermittent silences the vowels and
their macron the consonants elided
into a deep wood the demesne of
deluded Persephone and mirrors
elaborate with backward script which
is the origin of literature the backdrop
of rumor and hearsay naming gods
after the days of the week summering
in marble quarries mysterious with
the noise of statues coming into being

the reckless sun and the workshop
of sweat and chisel the profound face
of *Daedalus* striking the anvil and loud
dissension among the goddesses the prize
awarded after school to the lascivious
one whose shapely divinity thinly clad
in muslin and see through skin shining
like a planet wounded by an unknown
flame essence of the cosmos secret
and shifting from blue to red enormous
with number and nostalgia the going
home the close of day the hemlock and
myrrh and the mausoleum across
the way next to the civil war cannon
and the old court house hoosegow
for the town drunks and poets and
so it goes the kids ruminating over
the second cigarette of the hour
and placid detonations in the sky
just above their heads everything
turning to rock and gravity a drug
coursing through the veins a speed
and a depth to know and soon forget

08-14-21

UNIDENTIFIED FLYING OBJECTS
para mi hermano, siempre !

the time we invented the night skies
millions of rutilating coruscating revolving
galaxies which fit in the corner of an eye
nothing but a shivered mirror reflection of our minds
cascading and plunging through a miasma
of pre-birth and post-death experiences
even as implosions of grammatical fireworks
stretched the limits of thought to madness
the vibrating oscillating yet abrupt wavelengths
of light and air and breath and sensory projections

kinetic distortions of image and resonance
not of life but an imitation and repercussion
of memory in its enigmatic unraveling
through the labyrinthine corridors of a syntax
nothing more than a puzzle the ingrained copy
of an untranslatable text evolving and dissolving
simultaneously in the photomat of a five and dime store
near the connection of South Broadway and *hell*
and getting up from the dark grassy expanse
we pocketed suns and evanescent moons and
unnamed celestial bodies perilously proximate
to our own headrests of unequivocal stone
and assumed the day had no finite conclusion
though the black tide of an unresolved past
was soon enveloping us body and soul as we walked
backwards through a water of fireflies into a glass
which contained tiny evocations of insect monarchs
whose minute roaring deafened the possibility of light
wondrous moment of boyhood ! we were each other
both formal and irreversible unidentified flying objects !
who could recognize in us the innate need to be *other* ?
the ear was poetry in itself gathering in nocturnal
noises buzz and roll of mountain and crashing waves
seas of language descending from the momentary heavens
a plethora of words sounds syllables disconnected and
aggravated efforts at articulation a heaving tempest
of descriptors and valueless punctuations the *Poem*
as it came to be an issue of screens and painted fans
recollections of a single moment carved in dust
atop the pyramid of the sun the greatest of eternities
see *us* ambling slowly homeward beings of a music
that lacks retaliation and echo frail anatomies
disjunct consonants evaporated longing
invisibly ascending into the massive tide-pool
of asterisks and stellar placenta distance and augment
of oblivion the reverse of time on its wheel
unidentified flying objects !

08-15-21

THE FALL OF *KABUL*

carpet-baggers locusts cannibals lice
the head turns to stone the moon is drawn
out of its well and decapitated in a dust flurry
minutes before the evacuation promises of
paper-flowers fruit without vermin *bread !*
for two decades a series of statues come and gone
artillery composed of offal and headwinds
ox-carts bearing sultans of medieval dialects
everything a matter of renunciation
movies cosmetics opium military footwear
the greatest Demon in the world has just
surrendered his vices in a big photograph swap
history is written on mattresses with bedbugs
remember the Soviet carrion ?
remember the big Buddha at Bamian ?
five thousand years since the Aryans bruited
the Vedas in the Hindu Kush and today
nothing but a reversal of system and value
blond poster-girls peeling off bloodied walls
hoodwinked soldier boys from Iowa City
haunted by the part they played
dismembering the carcass of progressive Reform
Jihad ! Mujahideen ! turn the volume up !
the Twin Towers were destroyed by fireflies
a nuisance of idioms and heresy
monstrous illiteracy of social media lies
verbiage and tattooed air multiples of Zero
Balkh the birthplace of Rumi surrenders !
President of USA suffers from PTSD
a painted screen a flutter of Chinese diplomats
wearing poisoned masks an x-ray of Night
what good are stealth bombers and drones ?
red ants versus black ants ! civilization !
mendacity of General Petraeus and the CIA
operatives who drill like moles through earth
nothing is solid and even less is holy
the Beloved ! houris wearing burkas on Main Street
Yea this day is Paradise and Gehenna
above and below and *forever !*

08-15-21

LOVE IN ITS FINAL STAGES

the hesitancy of waking the shivers and cold
of space come down to a residual increment
between life and death the instant of eternity
for how many centuries does the single inch suffice
we intake breath release energy suffer grief
sleep on stone peddle lies in dreams of success
linger by the altar's chilled ashes trying to recall
the body that was sacrificed listening intently
for the siren to double the corner and the red
engines and the spark and intaglio of heaven's
faint promise will it revive will it survive will
it remember anything if it ever was and hands
shake intermittently searching for their shapes
shifting silhouettes brooding on stucco walls
by the plum tree near the excess of gravel and
the painted stones and the wheels coming home
an evening of impermanence the grammar of
asterisk and portfolio and nothing to offer
the bruised parenthood but errors of childhood
rumor and resonance of planetary lives myths
that haunt mountains and dialects cities that
lace earth like garlands turning on its axis daily
what are the demarcations of time ? a week ?
a month ? the rotations of satellites and copies
of distance and echo misplaced ciphers on disks
rock formations and oracles fuming disregard
of intellect and the serpentine conclusions to
battles and broken treaties and pollution as
it envelopes the noosphere and idioms argue
this side or that side and north plunges from
its place and south divulges its countless dead
who is right is never wrong and go in circles
the blind rishis the seers in their Vedic babble
issuing small footnotes to the Invisible text
consulted in bathrooms or tossed into dumpsters
the garbage of civilization worm-eaten wrath
teeming with linguistic decay madness addiction
the descriptors of a syntax of mutilation and
blind devotion love in its final stages yearning

memory riddled with mistaken exits the detours
and shuttles of thought having no place to turn
yawning abyss of progress & manifest destiny
insect caravans of philosophy totter veering
off the cliff of conjecture and quantum mechanics
do the numbers add up ? are we awake or only
in a trance of pronouns and stolen identities ?

08-16-21

THE DEATH OF *HECTOR*

so saying glorious Hector his arms reaching
but holds naught but phantom words gone
fluttering into the dusk and sea-shore's vain
rushing against the tide whispering asterisk
the pale and flickering overhead and grief
uppermost in the socket and spear and the
length of time once seemed infinite now but
a breath's throw away from stone and shaking
the horse-hair crest a shadow before memory
of the child affrighted left behind in the nurse's
bosom her well-girt waist and noisome hair
loosed the shapes of yearning and loss but
hear ! tears spent in the dark and pillow
the suffocated moan alas ere Troy its last
fulfills sundered into burning dust and woe
all mysterious the oracle and the distances
of the immortals lounging afar in mansions
of light and what they bring about arguing
and envying mortals and cast cups half-full
aside and dominate the atmospheres wrathful
thunder strokes the lightning of cinema and
repercussion time after time the dread and
dying soon Hector nine times his round
about the quaking walls of the citadel
his end the rout of verse and wailing

08-16-21

THE SIMPLE EFFORT OF BECOMING

who we are is a matter of conjecture
does existence depend on correct pronunciation
or the equitable distribution of pronouns ?
or is language itself the error and deception ?
syllable after syllable echo after echo
dream-speech statue-talk the voluble flight
of vowels into the ether tap tapping on tables
for a word with spirits and the consonants
that compose them and the cinema of shadows
plethora of science-fiction and ideology
hands can only reach so far and feet can
only move in circles so many times before vertigo
takes the body from its self plunging it
into some oneiric cavity and days are but
a fugue of nomenclature and number a chaos
meant to represent order a phenomenology
of light and metaphysics a set of theories
about divinity immortality salvation and
finally nothingness which surrounds all activity
being and repercussion of being illustrated
by fictions of air trade-winds and blows
of celestial bodies against one another the *gods !*
we look askance awkward expressions of noise
communication between two tin-cans
long afternoons which last half a lifetime
called childhood when without thinking
everyone is assumed to be somebody else
playthings discarded toys memories of the *before*
unexpectedly grief interpolates its literatures
days no longer seem to be separate but collapse
into a module of repetition and confusion
was the same yesterday the same as tomorrow ?
longing and the poetry of leaf and stone
the eclipses of mind and the abyss forlorn
in which the controversy of ourselves darkens
inexplicable letters glyphs runes photo-clips
we are in love ! it aches to be ! texts run on
about the founding of cities of epic battles of sand
and insect caravans drawing across the brain

futile renditions of an apostrophe or an asterisk
conjunctions have no value ! isolation and madness
the sole properties that ultimately define us
moving in incrementally incomplete gyres
writing what cannot be recalled
wax figurines fragments of a puzzle
learning to read and forgetting to read
signatures of interchangeable symbols
strokes that vanish no sooner do they occur
inks and the diapason of the unheard Note
whispers across the greater waters of time
that never reach the ear
we are no longer home

08-17-21

BEAUTIFUL GAME
Madonna Louise Ciccone August 16, 1958

you're 63 now ! beautiful inch of photographed flesh
reconditioned transmogrified duplicated multiplied
how many times will you traverse the camera's eye
to satisfy some plethoric notion of yourself ?
there can be nothing real about this synthesis
and chemistry of copies replications and forgeries
the soul's ultimate paradigm in a cosmetics of sex
redundant revolving asterisk of a puzzled being
skin and essence perfume and adage of illusion
the hundred and ninety-ninth time I saw you
it was in a flashing automobile drawn by the sun's
exhausted steeds blackened by the warp of time
ray-of-light superimposed on an image repeated
in a thousand pages of fifty glossy magazines
each with an international edition in Esperanto
the dead language of Tuscany babble of garbled talk
gossip of gnats and termites internalizations of heat
going round the unfixed center of a discarded movie lot
sandstorm and fiction of punk garage sound nuisance
of noise battling the hair-do of a prima-donna from

the depths of a personal hell intaglio and bubble
floral pronoun dissolved in texts of magical impersonation
yourself done and undone in lingerie and lipstick
itching to transcend were it not for the hunger of fame
relic and illicit hyphen of boredom and choreography
you can't get much older ! surgery and pain-killers
desperation to outdo the shadow of your former self
bopping on the hairline of eternity with some doo-wop
cast-off figure eight of a boy who's taking you for a ride
some cheap millions of dollars a pose struck too often
alleyways of dark deceit ash-cans and art history
of a diorama with you exposed in the middle stripping
and undressing and disfiguring and cheating and lying
a literature of teasing and melodrama put to song
a wistful rendition a playback of stealth and rape
you can't do it no more ! streamlined color scheme
sunset trilogies Spanish pronouns of fate and guitars
electricity is the best thing you have going and adultery
yearning the days when you could beat a dime to the floor
this is no love poem no dumb troubadour bird-chirp
but the last link in a chain-letter that has been circling
the adolescent universe since I first heard you sing
dress you up in my love

08-17-21

HARMONIC CONVERGENCE (1987)

According to Argüelles, the Harmonic Convergence also began the final 25-year countdown to the end of the Mayan Long Count in 2012, which would be the so-called end of history and the beginning of a new 5,125-year cycle. Evils of the modern world, e.g. war, materialism, violence, abuses, injustice, oppression, etc. would have ended with the birth of the 6th Sun and the 5th Earth on December 21, 2012. This is not known to have occurred.

nine hell-cycles ended ! nine hell-cycles begun again !
to be sure history has completed its unfinished text
literature too has finalized its erroneous variation
does a thirteenth month add anything to the world's
wobbling off-axis trajectory toward auto-destruct ?

driverless trucks in New Mexico and drone-toys
taking picture of Mars' surface to what avail ?
Prophet *Valum Votan* could not push his respiration
beyond the mortal limits of Anno Domini 2011
six more suns ! five more earths ! unlimited Access !
photography is the reverse of immortality in a hyphen
tenth anniversary of Elvis Presley's overdose death
Cortés resurfaces in Disney World by the fountain of Youth
Montezuma ! Cuauhtémoc Cárdenas ! Trotsky !
drug cartels disappeared persons drive by shootings
the New World self-defined ! *la frontera del norte* !
there is no Peace in the Valley only a new Walmart
cordilleras paved over for swift super-roads leading nowhere
jungle rot brain fever license to kill on the spot
caravans of illegals from of all places Honduras !
Doris Day singing *Que será será* to Olmec morticians
Shboom Shboom ! life could be a dream sweetheart
Joe ! can you hear us ? New Year's Eve 2012 didn't happen
the oval office has been vacated twenty times over
the cities we designed on rolls of x-ray paper
have been atom-bombed in the foyer of the Mayo Clinic
and we still haven't figured out uses of the pluperfect
how does life come to be in an infra-red Big Bang ?
you eked it out one puzzling page after another
Yucatan and then Outer Space and cosmic shuttles
bearing the Maya with their hieroglyphs back to earth
you pressed the Pope to drop his way of fixing years
for your rabbit fox and running monkey version
do you remember the time you tried to wake me up
from my catastrophic near-death alcohol experiment ?
it was love that brought us together in a Chicago theater
and all those blues records we collected *Honey Behind the sun*
the religions that obfuscate men to commit horrors
have only intensified their lethal grip and the heat
has been turned way up and the oceans have lost it
coral has been bleached and three thousand species die a day
Joe , tell me it could have been different had the convergence
been less harmonic and more in tune with *Realpolitik*
were you already dead in 1987 and speaking from Beyond ?
you spiked your marijuana with oregano and lay back

giggling with Al Nugent in a 1961 Hyde Park basement
already a fermented noon was putting you on the Precipice
French expressionism neo-Platonic gaggle avant-garde
you knew it was all an academic hoax the world of letters
Teotihuacan Chichen Itza and Lomas Chapultepec
the claustrophobic immensities ! Time unraveling
around the puny remnants of the sun and its pyramid
++
the pitiable sack called mind has earned its dust

08-18-21

WHAT IS THE PRICE IN TEARS ?

this small thing called earth faint of and pigment
leaf and broken branch echo and effigy of noise
we have ceased feeling eye and ear grown dull
by traffic of unmeaning the seized soul uttering
names of wordless content the long and flickering
structure of air with its immense architecture
yearning and pale the faded blooms of thought
archaic sorrows like a black mass of waters
rising from a sea far to the west of the mountains
in dales and crevices a wilderness of undergrowth
a lack of sense as clouds mushroom orange and black
in the southern latitudes if only a cry from the alphabet
a surmise of consonants and vowels made to sound
like appeals from the Vault and small excesses
of light that hit the pavement with the hint of days
to come leaving behind those that passed unremembered
on high coruscating celestial morphs like signals
meant to be read but never understand the meridian
and its aftermath spilling out over the courthouse yard
and the civil war cannon and the voices of adolescents
in search of their partners within volumes of
unedited pages blanks and fuses and distances
if only the doors to the library could open effortlessly
instead the steps keep increasing and the offer of smoke
or the indignation of unfinished marble and a hand

that descends mysteriously to part the ways and Loud !
pronunciations from the past ancient arguments
divided between circumflex and tonic accents
the instantaneous appearance of a text to be memorized
before sundown and the rush to the drugstore where
the kids in small groups huddle over a glass to read
but it is not possible the graphemes and hiatuses
have been wired the wrong way and the modern age
so promising in electricity and speed and comfort
dispels nothing of the innate grief the broken promise
of breath and health and the unexpected as always
occurs and they stand in awe and gaze at the body
grown smaller now and prey to convulsions and trance
long are the minutes between cognition and its loss
weeping does nothing to mitigate the lament of sirens
the bed-sheets yellowed with sweat and the angels
at the window pounding their wings uselessly
this small thing called earth faint of hue and pigment

08-19-21

THE BUTTERFLY'S THRENODY

the end never comes at the right time
plangent willows fragments of a stream
written in corrosive subscript a whispering
between letters saddening a length of air
pale green and the swinging drone of locusts
shadows plunging through fields of corn
the least is fox-fire a small decay of winter
tassels of cloud drifting through sleep's dusk
then I saw Max standing bodiless in the sky
not a tale of pollen and golden incrustations
nor of jeweled cities too marvelous to describe
but winged phantoms of bee and hummingbird
the lark that reaches for the highest note
branches trembling with the weight of dew
and a vista of garden and mold and trembling
grief afar and near the distances of sorrow

the monarch's painted wing the ants who
mine decay and dung the ancient airs of
fragrance and melody but a single sob
the mother of antiquity draped in cinders
the bush and plot where roses wither and die
the setting sun to never rise again the orb
of cosmic satellites blackened in a crisp
the crematorium's infinite harp plying its
credo in unum deum to ears of monophonic chant
alas the longest way is never to get home again
the gravel and riddled rocks and heavens
haunted in the glint of broken glass and kites
that surge in a southern breeze when death
in her polychrome luster of parade and signs
brings to everyman a play of human ruin
the mind in all its unsettled flights broods
and creates its butterflies to make amends
for its countless error and sin the freighted
molecule of thought the abyss eternal of
never waking and from a mountain replete
with vanishing springtimes resounds the knell
the clinic's late afternoon carillon allure
and sympathy for those who went before
all is accident and unexpected sickness
a bed of short-lived blooms and leafage
and soil and rain that hastens destinies
whose illusive patterns entice memory
to repercussions of insect drum and flute
then I saw Max standing bodiless in the sky

08-21-21

ORPHIC STROPHE

a few rocks moving in the wild
and where I step no earth to land
the sound of memory hidden in crevices
or the lauds and symphonies of a broken lute
the choirs and effigies of wandering verse
lament and systole for one gone missing
in the long ago of texts that none can find
how great the immensities of atmosphere
dense the dusks and enmities of the poets
envy the stricken note and fiercely noisome
the seas that vex the ear in its grandiose snare
to hear once again the purities the essence
of ether and in between the echo of vowels
a retribution of language in its tangled
dialect of hill and demesne of undergrowth
the place I shift my shadow is the other bank
of the rushing Stygian stream the blank
and fuse of issuing gasolines and oils
to burn eternally the simple savaged mote
the hands that plied the loom and combed
the raveled mass of morning hair are past
and everywhere the unfocused eye travels
nothing but weeds and consonants forlorn
and absence of shadow and clarity
and the Vault where a thousand asterisks
flicker in the inch of a flashing universe
night ! the vast and hollow space
the ravaged dark and untenanted house
where used to play the game of cheat
and kiss the Beloved's destiny
to have dared look back and turned
to eternal stone the embodied silhouette
her fingers her waist her tiny fluted cries
her Spain of endless longing
now lost in a hemisphere of leaves
that by day's end forever close
their hoarse and plaintive dialogue

08-21-21

THE BUDDHA'S DREAM OF MIND

the conventions and signals that diametrically oppose
and the heavens in their silent choirs and embolisms
earths multiplied where emptied souls walk and
wonder what is this place of ash and smoke
this desert blessed by simoom and ravaged silk
stone signed by the nautilus and rocks in ferment
a legend was written here in meters of soundless note
the message of here and after the hint of other pasts
why did we not listen ? blood was in the plaintive cry
a child was buried in the shadow's distant city
four and five the number of unknown truths
succor was in the wine-red tresses of the woman
who undressed her skin of its fortitude and charm
disembodied the ruins of warriors loaded on to carts
drawn by donkeys and heading to the wasted south
bereavement and enmity the distinctive marks they wore
none could stop by the pliant trees nor from wells
draw water to bless the day and hundreds by the thousands
of demons and imps in clusters glorious as flies
of bright emerald and flashing swarms of sunlight
yet blackened in the unslaked minute of memory's
fragmentary recall when we were alive and learned
to read by numbers and thrive on purloined merchandise
statues appeared out of nowhere in symmetries of sand
and noontime gestures and birds and crocodiles and
elephants of royal gait the plaza tramped and filled
with rile and wailing and cacophony to figure out
who was first in the mortal race and who was second
from the last the sad and wistful cadaver in tow
laid on its barge of roses and windows that opened
loud on the vertiginous assault of breath and a Buddha
the once and only of his kind surrounded by wrecked
automobile parts and discarded templates of time
arose in saffron pleats and starvation to lift his finger
the index of sublime repercussion and pronounce words
inaudible about the hour to follow and laid his stone
upon the head of a roadside clerk and in speech
of fern and dichotomy proceeded to unravel the Law
laying his great corpse down on the Antarctic map

to sleep the endless syllable of space and dream
that once upon a time the world was fresh and warm
a blank land of shapeless mountains and undivided seas
a season when mortals grew like spores of greenery
until one day with bomb in hand the Enemy approached
denying all that was predicted and spat out his bile
and wound serpents around his temples and declared
an End to all that was and all that would ever be
begin again if you can this blasted dream of Mind !

08-22-21

UPON HEARING OF JACK HIRSCHMAN'S DEATH

I am having a dream that I never was
between the ears a nothing void a blank
that supersedes all other blanks like
hearing about the death of another poet
so easy to report you want to deny it
could be my demise as well unknown
in a suburb of latin hexameters a loud
but incessant silence pursuing a funnel
deep within the left year that I never was
in this dream of subtle and querulous demons
adolescent misfits in alcoholic trousers
or teasers with hair of fiery plumes and
pizza lipstick-gloss whose ever haunting
photos are pasted in the brain's back-room
lights off no visible horizons tantalizing
tickle of hair brushing the nerve-tips
to sleep forever in the demesne of Rajas
and chrome-plated grammarians whose
task is to lift the accent off every known vowel
and the absurd but infernal sub-text lingers
doubt that anything was ever written correctly
transpositions of consonants and envelopes
addressed to the dead-letter box and fogs
rolling across the Golden gate and into a
Vallejo street address where a Nisei woman

lies pondering the Sacred Heart a well
of half-taught learning syllables in red ink
posters and rocks tamed for their license
to throb and so much else on the edge of
eternity dream I am having I never was
not even as the split zygote that woke up
speaking Mexican to the appeals court
in a court-house the size of Olympus and
whetstone and dialect talking backwards
to the one-eyed love the step and cigarette
of thirteen Moon the chasuble spilling
its oneiric ambrosia liquor of the gods
in their so-called fame and relentless
debauchery and all the transpired beauties
the wired mechanics of a city built on the third
rail demolition and exercise of memory
wearing hounds-tooth jackets reciting as
ever the unfinished and unvarnished verses
derived from Li Po and submitted to
the headmaster of a reform school for failed
artists the barking and tremulous soprano
of a voice disembodied for its heat and value
I am having that never was a dream within
a dream an illegible pill dissolving like
light on the far side of a sun blackened
in mourning for still another poet or child
a grace to have lived and died in the *Word*
not the logos but the untrammeled lyrics
of those for whom Bedlam is a sanctuary
a lotus pond a refuge at the bruised feet
of the Buddha of Bamian exploded
into fragments of air bliss ever sounding
in the enormous repercussion of space
a dream I never was and am still having

08-23-21

THE NOTION OF LIFE ETERNAL

"ma ricorda che tu sei qui solo per essere odiato,
per rovesciare e uccidere"
    Pier Paolo Pasolini, Teorema

is this life the gift of a previous infinity ?
momentous and infernal instances of a light
that seems to come from nowhere and to limit
our vision to the outlines of motion and gravity
characteristics of being mortal and forever
adolescent in the intent to survive and understand
cars come and go the latest models and cigarettes
invented for the pure devilment to impress
and ladders that succumb at the first step
plunging the unwitting soul into a private hell
mixture of dream and trance called experience
each of us is the illusion of a separate pronoun
a talking jabberwocky speaking endless nonsense
to a mirror figure in search of a shadow and
landing In a corn-field and listening to the shrill
Gregorian chant of cicadas and waiting for some
Buddha or other to arrive head-first in the context
of language and salvation denoting syllables
as they chance in the long unraveling of the *dharma*
the choice is never ours ! we are all bhikkhus
mendicants thirsting for the unknown and impossible
to reunite memory to its hallucinatory other *oblivion*
passing from hand to hand unrequested bodies
names and addresses of perishable entities
and this Buddha will preach something indefinable
that can never be translated by the human ear
and stones will lie down and waters will lift
their elegant mansions into the blazing sun
yet nothing will have transpired but the minute
signal of time passing through its own eye
long summers will have occurred in that instant
conflagrations of grass and childhoods too
memorable to bear and the sick-bay and the sacred
crematoria where statues are purified of their longing
and it is ever the individual   who must suffer for
his solitude and to sleep outside the year

forgetting the previous infinity whence he arose
in birth pangs and immemorial speech acts

08-23-21

TO BEGIN BY ANNOUNCING THE FORM

extreme thunders dark turbulence envy
of the worlds lightning and repercussion
time at a standstill the adolescent geographer
ruminating on his next Friday and the dress
and hair-style and lip color and ointments
her perfumes and drug of rumor and embossed
stitches on the side of the moon least visible
and suddenly speaking Latin and uttering
profanities of unrivaled elegance our hero
well-met in his fifteenth year and learning
to smoke and read Greek imitating awkwardly
the speech of Achilles or Apollo oracular
debates with the self about the self and
future positions of planet Mars in case of
love in the third degree ah ! so life begins
its wayward paths its treks through dialects
understood only by mountains and listening
to the night foliage to the leaves that anticipate
language foibles and follies of exaltation to
heights where white-armed Juno splendid
in her ire displays wrath in forty hues from
red to vermillion and carmine evoking seas
to roil and pant lashing the intrepid but ill-
framed barks of Ulysses or Jason and the winds
let out of their bag and swirling in the head
like a tempest in the labyrinthine cinema
starring Ariadne and her magic thread and
dreams of slaying the Minotaur or turning
into Bacchus on the isle of Naxos ivy-girt
profoundly drunk with eyes that only gaze
inwards toward the India where time is born
and eons pass in the minutes it takes the mirror

to disregard itself and swiftly combing and
buttoning and polishing and out the gate
in a music of electric guitars and drums
our hero the boy bard swarming with vowels
of creation and on his way through Elysium
to motels and resorts turns on his lantern
and through the byways of old Arcadia and
pretending to *know* seeks the outer cause
of things the essential and quintessential
Pythagorean and Platonic both and arrives
at the door that will never open and begins
to read his first and only poem

08-24-21

HEARTBREAK HOTEL

memory is on recall ! look at the streets
first it's springtime then summer and now autumn
kicking up the leaves by the curbside and sensing
the end of everything in the nip of the Canadian-sent air
there will be a celebration somewhere and apple cider
and horses champing in the barns and rivers flowing
backwards into the birth of ice and skies great
with the mnemonics of cloud and distance
a season when colors are brighter than ever and fast
sleeps the grass in its dream of winter in the tropics
ants crickets angle-worms that writhe underneath
lawns littered with over-ripe plums and the trees
each with a soul ! teaching and being taught
the rules of metamorphosis and simply put
the mind ! activities that turn night into the universe
brilliant pageant of stars and galaxies and pyramids
dancing with fireflies and screens in a language
that has yet to be invented and perfumes and hair
softened by a lilac sprig and fictions first encountered
in the marble pages of the enormous library
located next to the clinic and the drugstore and
the mysterious and darkened pool halls and bars

on Broadway where farmers in faded denim chew tobacco
will we ever learn how ? this is eternity here and now
the world pivots in the pupil of an eye fixed on light
in its vast and multiple directions and soon
it is the first day of something doors swing open
and shut glee-noises shouts and shoes and shirts new
and starched and who knows what will happen
when the next bell rings it will be full and metallic
and the sound of motors driving east to cities
fabulous and dirty with mills and errors and smoke
we are growing up ! we are emotions and alcohol
we place trust in hills that soon become snow fortresses
where we glide and triumph on fleeting toboggans
but when will we stop ? it is a radio and phonemes
in the air that recite invisible echoes of Latin
snatches of ribbons and gifts from the gods in the shape
of vowels and rearranged consonants and we make
what we can of the little speech we understand
and look to the day when we will be great as poets
making noise and sounds of rumor that reach the moon
but sleeping we know of accidents and the sickness
unto death the slowly unwinding film of the future
warning us that waking is dangerous and breath
everything is just barely visible on the *other* side
hunger ! maps and asterisks and the pantomime
of love so much exuding itself through the portal
cigarettes and voyages to the vast southland
staggering with its Aztec architecture and cordilleras
the very outcome of thought and imagination
come home ! address the nature of space and time !
how much is algebra and how little is Spanish ?
it's all an enigma a passing succession of effigies
but when will we stop ?

08-24-21

IF I SHOULD DIE BEFORE I WAKE

don't know what room I'm in bed covers rolled
back is mother coming with the ginger ale to bring
down fever or the tray with rice pudding and something
else I can't remember is the darkening by the window
odor of sulfa the tree branch scraping stucco just
outside a radio with noise of distance do I know
their names do I remember who and the street
is silent waiting for its lamps and the rubber tires
that make rumors of anxiety if it is home and late
already the night suppose it won't be tomorrow
again just the infinite reckoning inside the walls
to separate heat from its planet of origin going
in circles where the book left its page in isolation
the copper-colored print of warriors with spears
rising from earth how loud they have become like
the Mandan Indians on a bluff above a body of water
we don't really know how and what the doctor said
it may be seventy years later with windows that
look out on tobacco leaves and still without exact
science to explain why the process is aging mute
and irreversible to read between the sheets stained
with epic passages in Sanskrit at last which has
been studied and regulated the basis of religion and
philology more than the Ionians and Pythagoras
what school did I attend which was the teacher
who never raised her voice in the cattle raid of
the Greeks using long tablets with inscriptions
sometimes backwards and the mirror with its
possessive hyphens I think it was a mistake and
the drug ascending through chakras and the eye
composing light in its variables sometimes even red
the pigment that slowly dissolves in a drop of alcohol
pure as the saints and bonzes who live matted hair
and mostly naked in the jungles of the Deccan
far from this quandary of existence if I should
die before I wake the prayer goes round and wheeling
the deliberate syllable AUM into an ear the size of
a canyon whizzing and buzz of souls lost in the ether
where I flung the ashes learning to fly forgetting
to pray I am even as absent as those

08-25-24

AN EXPLANATION

the antique crater whose surging is vaster
than itself a quotation sleepless as hemispheres
in peril may be juxtaposed to big and blooming
bursts of flame and burnished plate to go phases
of a distant satellite lunation divisible by three
and the doubled consonant held like lapis lazuli
in the teeth is venom any worse is the noose held
by *Yama* god-of-death then as mortals walking
unawares in sunlight and all experience seems
as joy and benign a fiction of celestial thoughts
abstractions of echo and hue you paint me and
I'll do you the lovers twain in their unconscious
longing to die the exertion of sound in the second
degree the unexpected chasm the veritable fear
sleep brings on pierced by its glass of reduplication
how to wake from the dream we are having of
being and nothingness the empyrean of asterisk
devotion and desecration in the mind's gallery
of things desired and memorable for their
pleasure is yet a painful and dubious mirror
of the self boomeranged by its own pronoun
an artifact or bone-text the first attempt to play
with noise and assemble the varieties of meter
and poetry is the fix that brings hallucinatory
gods in their astral nomenclature impediments
to reason a fiercely adoring idea to have
what can never be possessed a photographic
reunion with time accidents of error and rumor
the world is not as big as imagined a spinning
and dizzy toy out of control in its projection
through gravity and anti-matter a spot on the
retina darkening the ink of perception out of
focus the other hemisphere rock fragment and
passion to know the seasons and their colors
and the number it takes to remember anything
borrowed footnotes from archaic inscriptions
alphabets and chisels and the fondness to record
moments of ecstasy and grief is called act of
creation numbing seconds to go before the whole
thing explodes the vertiginous monument of light
when leaf devours and is devoured by silence

08-26-21

ON THE THRESHOLD

take the trip that ends
solemnities rites vowel formations
rock and cliff roiling seas that
surround copies of matter mountains
like consonants juxtaposed to mountains
that merely exist in the mind's western quarters
the trip that ends somewhere in the middle
of the puzzle the unexplained and raffled thoughts
that end just before death's blank syllable sounds
echo and rotation of breath that ends
no sooner does day break over fossil dew
and outlines of leaf-shadow and the child
inside the fog-horn that eerie signal
across the darker waters of memory
ending in the vicinity of the forgotten script
bone-text and waxen seals the symbols
of horse and flame and things that appear
in the sky for no reason and end going to bed
one last time unknowingly and the switches
that go off on the walls and the windows
that shut of their own accord and outside
the sound of footsteps on the flower-bed
and the orient where the heavens burst
forever and a day in instants that implode
in canyons of air and repercussion and stain
on the marble hallway and the stairs
that never finish no more than the smoke
unwinding from the source of time
that ends

08-27-21

AN EPITAPH FOR JOSÉ

I question the sepulcher for its dignity
for its grammar and for its distance
for its inscriptions in silence and aphasia
I question the footpath and the stairwell

the flower-formations at the end of sleep
the distinctions between death and heaven
I question the silhouette and its shadow
the mirror that only contains absence
the photograph and its inconstant symbol
of negativity and reduction I question even
the accolade of statues and the southern hemisphere
where the dead go re-routed from the echo
and breath of memory and what is to question
of the inch that is the measure and the depth
and the tumbler of water where earths drown
I question the waking and the walking of
the daily man the hegemony of illusion and
power that hangs by a hair in the hurricane
I question the cathedral of doubt the hagiography
of stone-masons and the parallel lives of fossils
I question childhood and existence and fate
the tomb and the thimble and vessel of blood
I question history and gravel and motors
that copy the minds of angels and noise
the very apex of syllabic decay the hiatus
and number it takes to look into the *other's*
eyes and speak not in refrains but in width
I question the library and myth and afternoons
and I question heat because of the clinic and
the geminated consonant the birth of twins
the very certificate of written discourse
the asterisk and its cosmos rutilating
in eternally burning ethers and the hospital
I question for its domain of religious cant and
what else but the hill and its tangent and
to question the city is to surrender hope
smoke and chastisement of vowels darkness
forever questionable and the leaf and
finally grass that lies down evenings and
yearns for the finger gone lost in its winter
and the brother who is no question at all
but the riddle of infinity and error

08-28-21

BEDLAM : WHERE SUMMER IS FOREVER

summer afternoons when one eternity follows another
into the swimming pool of memory incarnadine instants
when decades collide with decades aging and going
backwards in time and surmounting the stone that
dominates the junction where east goes south and
multiples of sky crackle with pronouns of lightning
faces merge with mirrors and masks remain attached
to personae and the dramatist of the ego suffers amnesia
poles apart from the indigo error of a distant morning
alert with the traffic of hills and paleontological rumors
meridians of blazing infinities each briefer than an instant
passing in review the existential hues the divisive vowels
and corollaries the injunctions of hyphen and ampersand
bitter disputes about the way home through farmlands
devastated by intensities of heat and repercussion echoing
the ecstasies of the redundant game of numerical error
when windows replace windows with a dizzying alteration
of sound and gravity insanely pursuing each other in
a glass just out of reach of sleep and its insect oracles
noontimes and anvils that ricochet with nascent planets
comets with the gorgeous hair of adolescent girl-goddesses
skin and allure of the mysteries exhumed by fireflies
the day before yesterday which always follow tomorrow
and naps suffocating in puerperal cribs and alcohol
repeating in the language of trance and abscess an alphabet
whose first and last letters belong to mercury and iodine
utter confusion of the date and day of the week and month
sweating out a confession for a crime that never was committed
and the civil war cannon and the sloping lawns of gesture
and infamy the impious adjective of the judge in his homophone
dictating the course of the sun as it declines into aphasia
not to understand to confound top from down to look for
the switch on a non-existent wall the crumbling stucco
of a Sargasso sea whose circular and hypnotic lullaby
imitates the unending cycle of summer afternoon eternities

08-29-21

NIGHT ALONE IS A VISION

the incessant inch that separates memory from
its glassware and reflections the copies of planets
that harrow the mind before dawn's fierce abscess
each a dialect and idiom of untranslatable sounds
I am Ajax ! the spear cries hurtling through the brain's
right arm and suffer the little dust to endure the light
ancient and sorrow as it is the whole cannot be less !
poetry is the monograph of repetition and plagiarism
fixities of vowel traveling the wrong way to southland
and iterations of goddesses in the key of delta and
the furtive rotations of their eyes in ire and absence
an oath a sworn allegiance a broken promise skies
and meteors that destroy in a minute their fiction
who can ever sleep once the revelation manifests
darkness and the leaf that speaks of eternal space
the edges of a water that is mysteriously missing
and the bards and seers and rishis and poets all
the fakirs and nuisance of salesmanship of the deity
bread for those who make noise in a different tongue
for whom understanding is an escape valve a throne
as empty as the consonant that ends all words
four is not a number ! labyrinths and omegas fused
to the image of gravity as it descends from its echo
devaluation of statues millions of jewelry thought !

08-29-21

FOSSIL CONSONANTS

insect cuneiform of thought the ancient
and hierarchies of the invisible and invariable
sounds issuing from the buried voice of Achilles
how futile the few and perfected entities who
claim the prize of literature yet how insistent
the plaintive howl from beyond the tomb and
hosts of words doing battle with biblical foes
one-armed and with a command of language
that defies reason and no wonder ! skies
blacken with weaponry of diphthong and circumflex
and if there are children who belong to memory
their mouths are absent and yet how loud !
suffer the denizens of midnight soil dreams
and entelechy of the unforeseen encounter
 each is greater than the last and moons
twenty-nine in number quiver in an atmosphere
scintillating with mercury and quinine
some doppelganger is rising above the crest
and mountains the size of ampersands and
direction the full quantity of mind ! lessen
and quick the souls divagating in the wheel's
oriental path massive rotations of consonants
fossil rock solutions to the meaning of time
how immense the first word is ! and none who
recall its pronunciation and the vain tribes
of men in search of a Buddha to restrain them
vagrant anacolutha symptoms of parental disorder
violations of rite and statue the fastened grass
of the archaic darkening and still come evening
it is with faint trepidation the leaf appeals
to the oracle of oblivion and the greenery
that twines the vacant brain with repercussion
and sensation before the endgame
such is my heart ! gone !

08-30-21

A DATE WITH POETRY

and me standing there beneath the shield
of the world waiting in the prospect of you
coming back from the awning all text and glory
founding a city under the skin I who was
a member of no clan a justification to write
probing tongues alien and other of centuries
that flap like paper pages in the unwinding
width of time the metronome of memory
I look up and through the plate-glass
where mannequins exercise breathing half-
dressed their limbs what is the reason it
remains an abstract issue after school and
me standing there obeying no prosody or
grammar the rules of afternoons growing
up synthetically a fuse an hour just gazing
or glaring the optics of shadow and heartbeat
following with hungry eyes the skit of girls
in their crockery and cosmetics the plaid
of indifference as they swirl like blossoms
what did they know of Ovid or for that matter
India the replica of Spain in a diorama spun
by bee-swarms the delight of hair and comb
similitudes of sea and graphic pronouns
loosely pinned to cloud evocations in transit
mind a field of disordered consonant clusters
fame would be something if it weren't for
the safety pin holding chaos in place the vowel
of fabric and eau-de–cologne defining shoulders
for their intrinsic nudity and what of the movies
we're late and the strange thing is the mirror
where horse and rider collide in anticipation
of Fate's undeserving hand the isolation and
fusions of mouths darkening in a kiss

08-30-21

ODE TO THE NUMBER THREE

Hector adest secumque deos in proelia ducit
                    Ovid, Metamorphosis, XIII, 82

the catastrophe comes in threes one part illusion
two parts hallucination mind sets mind on edge
individuals as such crawl over the screen the flood
and passage to darkness and the salvation by rope
who knows what that means reiterating a finger
lost in evening grass a hunch this has happened
at least once before the invention of the lawn-mower
with her black nail-polish the intervening goddess
her fluted robe of savaged silk in ribbons a-flutter
her moon face the oval of desire in whole numbers
gilded around the sides a tripartite thought about
the end in syllables the brain has trouble deciphering
alpha of course but beta and gamma the third letter
of the self the quotient and amnesia of the every day
such as we are the storms and tempests the crashing
of the rule of three the nines and what they amount
to sections of antiquity passed around for inhalation
wild ! multiples and sequences of leaf and tarmac
the flight of the invisible and the tarrying parlor
where marble comes to life and talking makes it so
again the swift and its lumber and circling quoits
above their heads the religious antidote to fear
what is it but a flame that soon goes out the *Dice !*
levitation ! temptation ! three hemispheres in all
I am Viceroy of Peru since the world began !
the gods drawn into battle by Hector for what ?
mortal versus mortal in the eye of the hurricane
category three making landfall next Tuesday
when the horizon has been obliterated and there
they are runts and squatters of the human condition
pretending electricity won't go away and life eternal
for once the library is wrong and the shelves empty of
their puerile content illustrated matter in hieroglyphs
dragons and lemurs with human voices and threats
to atom bomb cities where they manufacture x-rays
why isn't this the last letter to be used ? ever !
of what use is *Three ?* there are cathedrals where

shadows clamor for a scrap of number for a side
to one of the triangles for a climb up the pyramid
there are kids named Joe for whom the sanctum
is always triple and the door has no reversal
up they all go the kid named Joe and his multiples
dividing three into Infinity and silence breaks in two
alone darkening with its single leaf and poetry

08-31-21

THE DIALECTIC OF LIGHT
"ubi nunc facundus Ulixes?"
                Ovid, metamorphosis, XIII, 92

to continue the questioning in sums of zero
left and right of the external hyphen and
its attributes the forged lambda and tau
to unlearn how to sleep and keep to rocks
and the pre-history of sound and grammar
iotas and thumbnails painted rust-black
glamorizing the goddess in her silhouette
shifting back and forth between asterisks
because of sky because of grass and death
what lies beneath the pronoun what wavers
being inconstant in punctuation and thought
mind ! the first and the last of ancient doors
superlatives of alpha added to the unfounded
stone the place in time where the driveway
disappears in a gravel storm and night's
absent omega and if you ask whose is this
armor these arcane robes this rain-filled
helmet or who was it that stood for years
on this painted marble effigy of memory
duplicated or multiplied in photo-clips
now fading in the sliding terrain of thought
there is no thing as weight or size nor envy
which works in insect hemispheres no such
matter as what you're looking for nor
schemes that bring delta to the surface

and heavens deteriorating by the syllable
into crashing space the biggest whorls
that fill the eye yellow atmospheres of sand
circumlocutions about the birth of time
disease of language hiatus and detritus of
vowels noisy theories of the after-life
a tomb a leaf fixations and obsessions
to re-live to die absenting the self the hour
it takes to become a ghost a copy of some
other who never really was but the worst
is yet to come in dialects of *if* and distance
imagine ! children dismembered by light
            where now is eloquent Ulysses ?

09-01-21

LIPSTICK THE COLOR OF THE AUTUMN SUN
for Mary Lou Willard, r.i.p.

radiance ! sunspots darker than fever
heaven is just a disyllabic sound blackening
between dreams of identity and gravity
what is the sequel to existence ? silence ?
revolving pronouns masks lettered by vowels
unconditional surrender of grammar to chaos
Saturday night dance postponed until death
couples in their adolescent suspension of time
succumb to narcolepsy and obsession
listening with a third ear to the sound of distance
everyone endowed with speech turns to stone
utter and fabric and noise and relativity
like bee-swarms caught in the hair of Pallas Athena
waiting immobile in the tardy metal of memory
whoever declares to be first in the contest
of alphabets and chemistry whoever stumbles
both knees caught in the nets of aphasia
whoever cannot withstand speed and poetry
is nonetheless the loser in a throw of the dice
emulations of gods ! they wear skin inside out !

from among them the love that supersedes
steps out in a pinafore and discarded hair
talking is irrelevant and tortoise shell combs
the stairs fill with enigma and suppressed violence
motors guns excursions in the philosophy of water
hunting for the animal that was never born
I am Orestes ! ever the cry of the defeated
how is it anyone really has *being ?* sleep !
when so many have already died and the least
of them looking brighter than archaic dew
grass is the form of her mind shadows and eye-liner
approaching human destiny in its stolen car
racing toward the improbable consonant
that concludes all literature and *Bang !*
she has never been alive for how can one
be consoled by the dead ? on the bottom step
as there are no others the dreamer folds
in his lap the paper of secrecy and salvation
phantom aspirin demolition of the past !
for the first time she is wearing lipstick
the color of the *autumn sun*

09-02-21

INSCRIPTION FOUND ON A THUMBNAIL

I was sick yesterday with memory
infant terrors increased like silk curtains
immense clouds were missing from eastern skies
I did not summon the dead—they summoned me
there was occlusion in the grammar of their eyes
and a single syllable that defined what they heard
amid the great noise of their distant hills
I was wounded by memory's pale satellites
the vague and faded patterns of their silence
each provoking a separate consonant to echo
a fatal decision to first deny then embrace
whatever it was that aroused my indistinct person
there were empty lots where girls exchanged seasons

for the *one* autumn of eternity and breath
and the strangeness of going lost in someone's gaze
brick structures totemic streets and the infinity of trees
where to walk how to know where to spell *moonlight*
I don't need to say who I am if I have amnesia
poetry is the darkness between lives or
it is nothing but the light that passes understanding
multiples of my mirrored self a ragged youth a kid
a debacle in untied shoes and torn shirts
a stick figure wandering through *Purgatorio*
with a dead love on either arm a poppy-stained
thought a woven labyrinth of unfinished verses
I have never been but a fleeting instant of deception
myself the erosion and index of forgotten nights
spent in the conflagrations of lexicons and booze
passions ! submit to the decrees of the gods
unname Thyself ! I was not there when my twin was born
denizen of limbo foresight of death Opium !
perfumes and scandals and suppressed encounters
with versions of the *other* in high heeled shoes
too much is made of the reflected glass
the heights of the second step and its cigarette
rushing and rushing through grasses of evening
always in search of the indefinable *thing*
loss and longing evanescent copies of memory
what remains ?

09-03-21

BEE-STING

if ten and six and no space left
the wild extra vowel the excess
doubt life the cathedral of ruin
sense and sight and loss of thought
to fly ! aspire to colonies of grace
checkered inch of breath please
the fix and such as hair can comb
to be and then the brink and fall
five thousand nanoseconds blinking
what am I to you dear reader but
a blue *buzzing* book a fuse and tone
different languages colors fright
pages turned backwards at the corner
and drugs while trucking to the hills
if was never the following text and
blanks that flower on the back
of smoke the stairs that lead to
gasoline and dialects of despair
we wake ! to what ? the blaze
and tonic of consciousness too
soon filtered through darkness
wander the hand to look for sounds
for vehicles that lack names
phase the foot heal the knee soul
and wing the energies to die and
know the noun without a shape was
none but the leaf's silver silence

09-03-21

from **THE BOOK OF THE DEAD**

phases luck transience shining depths
sounds trance inevitable discoloration
spatial fugue elimination sonnet disrobed
vowel activity clenched fists overpowering
awesome distances hills dialects twilight
dying hands hips cleavage vales despair
odes tonic accent graphic mood hiatus
asterisks ampersands hyphenated breath
fingers grass darkness swelling bees hush
swarming pyramids southland juncture
soils grammar marble statuary speech
circumflex rotation lunar bedlam eyes
blackening homophones solar resonance
echoes futile aggravation hopeless ring
souls phantoms flight wings autograph
identity hollow cavernous hearing hive
memory again emblem planets plunge
redness oracle haruspex dictation *Lo !*
cadaver girlfriend cornfield motel high
deity treason breadth wrists tongs flesh
articulation persona mask copies effigy
silent consonants error bleeding rumor
bedside temperature fever darkening I
syntax fragment gravel paint illusory
length seas loud radio songs fireflies you
screens remote pages blank conjunctions
cold frame night swift clouds stellar sails
woven interstices bang plasma radiance
erased ego armless spear birds-eye bole
eternity trees longing punctuation fiercely
falling breathless imitation air storms and
but while why ice source skin touch failed
archaic stone glyphs hallucination death

09-04-21

NOSTALGIA

the thread is the melody and the houses
empty of their persons and dark with echo
how stone ! how absolutely gravel ! hues
of a redundant red the valley and dale
where tumble scores of missing notes
the great and aching song of silence and
woe the encapsulated mind ! greening as
eclipses of the moon hidden in cornfields
where it never stops being July month of
the antipodes and motels or it is a hard
walk home the long way down alleys and
shrubbery where the devil mixes souls
between Aztec and modernity turning
dog-eared pages with a fine tooth comb
the immensities ! how can night be so brief ?
kaleidoscope of eternity switching blades
resonance of hills buried in an arm of space
lifting cyclopean fragments out of a poem
written five thousand and eight years ago !
who can read *that* ? important to insert
commas out of place asterisks and dots
coded residue of the black hole discovered
on graduation day when Latin and diesel
fuel were raging tempests and seas new to
literature and the cinema of hair-line and
waste the very world a symposium of noise
to separate vowels from the chaff ! rock !
pomp and aphasia fossil rains poverty
give *them* bread ! ignition and science
kids tutored in obsession and honorifics
unattached wings circling Betelgeuse
phantoms of a short-circuited after-life
my brother ! dead of a late Tuesday hour
whenever grass is opprobrium and depth
he is there his wondrous fragrant head
and the sack full of dandelions a foot
at a time before it reaches China !

09-04-21

102

AT THE TEMPLE OF ARTEMIS, EPHESUS

what is to be given to the leaf but silence
the deadened end of sleep that never comes
heights of memory contained in the thumb
hip or knee of one who has disappeared over night
edges and fractions ! nothing is ever whole
nor grass running over its limit of decades
nor the temple ruin reclining in the heat of centuries
a book a script an index of homophones lost
to libraries now sunk in darkness of the ages
a light a fane a corresponding lantern
depths within a single inch of unrecalled distance
such and no more the smaller portions of air and cloud
the roaring none will ever hear and thunder of lapse
and renown just out of earshot the lawns
tumbled down hills of unrecorded dialects
so many the few ! what gift is one day more ?
dawns and echoes of coming forth and the barge
of paper flowers listing uselessly in the canal
and the overhead structures waiting for the collapse
in which one did the brother go missing ?
on what floor of the unplanned edifice of immortals
did children playing one afternoon simply vanish ?
great maps drawn and redrawn with red and blue lines
phases of an outdated moon on its knees peering
into the water that bears no reflection
the all is nothing ! playthings effigies copies of shadows
that went before unconscious of their destiny
one day ! and the next never comes

09-05-21

JOSEPH ARGÜELLES CLASS OF 1956

"Sì, certo, cosa fanno i giovani intelligenti,
delle famiglie agiate, se non
parlare di letteratura e di pittura?"
            Piero Paolo Pasolini, Teorema

this is forever ! I won't be back I won't sing
this is time out ! no numbers left to count
there's nothing outside of space but eternity
this is the big one ! don't think of me as gone
flowers and easels half-painted half destroyed
rooms and chambers and closets without doors
attics and basements with large black eyes
and lawnmowers and grass cut into heaps and
fingers gone into isolation and dandelions packed
into sacks at highway crossroads and walking
backwards home which isn't there and windows !
this is the last breath ! count me out and down
forget I ever was and talk no more behind my back
it's done and over it's a melody without notes
songs and reiterations and lonesome absences
of hills and sunsets on the snow and girls innocent
and sweet and lilac-spray and wan doe-like eyes
fireflies and screens ! dancing with empty partners
broomsticks and charades and second floor halls
where shadows twist and wind around themselves
mirrors and aspirin and cut me to the quick !
remember not to cry ! I just came and went like
a bullet in the dark all hair and pose and smirk
an alphabet without memory my mind on speed
whatever I touched was without matter a void
and trance the hallucination of a life's career
brush in hand and a motto to excel I spared
my twin the opposite direction and left hanging
shattered vowels in my wake x-rays of the air
in the end whatever painting I never finished
is what I bequeath an Aztec mask and distance
the length of the highway to Teotihuacan in 1953
I conquered the pyramids of Sun and Moon !
it was then I began to really die transformed
once and for all a pronoun that belongs to clouds

a face inverted person of two thousand mandalas
Valum Votan the wizard who painted calendars !
Joe as always standing on the outside looking in

09-05-21

VIDA ALUCINADA DEL PINTOR JOSÉ ARGÜELLES
para mi hermana Laurita

padre el policía Enrique Argüelles famoso por
sus reyertas y borracheras
madre la siempre ausente norteamericana
Ethel Pearl Meyer enferma de cigarillos y nieve
vocación desde niño pintor siguiendo los pasos
del padre el que vió los sesos del célebre revolucionario
Leon Trotsky en Coyoacán
lugar de nacimiento el Mayo Clinic
infancia de niño travieso el Distrito Federal
Mexicali Los Ángeles y luego el Mayo Clinic
donde empezó a ser delincuente y adolescente
pintando y abusándose con alcohol
educación La Universidad de Chicago donde
tomó su PhD en Historia del Arte tratando con
los Impresionistas franceses con quienes hablaba
como un chafado bajo la influencia de LSD
más tarde y después de muchos "viajes malos"
se reformó convirtiéndose en el profeta Maya Valum Votan
lo que sabemos de su persona desde la Convergencia Harmónica
es que ante todo fue un impostor sin sombra una máscara
un viajero en espacio y tiempo uno que jugaba
con ideas improbables acerca de la divinidad oscura
de las fechas totémicas del calendario maya
por su parte nunca dejó de pintar aunque hay muy poco
que queda de su obra no más vestigios de pensamiento
color de los campos de maíz del Mayo Clinic
fumaba marijuana y huyó de su país natal
para vivir como un Maori en Nueva Zelandia
murió de repente y misteriosamente un martes
en el estado de Victoria Australia un vagabundo

pero siempre con unas ideas lúcidas
esas estrellas verdes que le aparecieron una noche inolvidable
fuera del Mayo Clinic al lado de su gemelo
ya hace siglos y siglos

09-05-21

THE GEMINATED CONSONANT

to ponder and gain on night nothing but
ruins of syntax and unmeaning a slender
blade caught between grass and darkness
a distant echo yearns to be *other* and
at such depths it can only be a wound
brought from a previous world into this
a *one* suddenly reversed there can be
no higher number none but scattered
light shot through with enigma the holy
distance between eternity and the sudden
ending called memory something that
cannot be described segment of an hour
marked by indistinguishable sounds
hissed syllables sonant mysteries bound
to sleep's most profound labyrinth
signals dots ampersands asterisks hiatus
the geminated consonant buried in a leaf
agony of character a jig-saw puzzle of
islands in a painting of unnamed seas
beside a door that cannot open shadow
and silhouette erased inside the mirror's
oracular domain *then* a day occurs when
divided in two a body forms and has
hands and their circumference around
the solar disk deep breathing homophone
and desire one to the other speaks not
as statues or morals in a play but surprised
repercussion of effigies so like each other
they are a resemblance and an appearance
and walking the park's interminable length
tending to the wound within and speaking

as if glass and what it contains or the stars
that only approach at noontime the singular
inferences of death the inexplicable
how can it ever be that one will be without
the other in some future hologram mere
resonance of the time the gods allotted
to one or the other but to *which* ?

09-06-21

ANCHISES
(tanta homines rerum inconstantia versat)
Ovid, Metamorphosis, XIII, 646

whitening anemones from an unknown sea
my grief ! great invisible wings of air like
a dream and swooning blindly as swans or
butterflies out of a forbidden memory
skies redundancies of mineral oblivion
come and go sleeping noiseless antibodies
life ! the immeasurable content of mind
punctuating the empty spaces before and
after light and the birth of time and sound
whatever is sorrow whatever is pleasure
the moment of either is gone ! two is never
a number but a point of separation
majesties of the void ! to count and not
recall which is the rising cipher and
which descends to the bitumen pits of hell
it's all there in one aggravated moment
the discovery and the nadir of ignorance
why can't it stay put ? it does not redeem
there is no way out but the unconscious
exit through the small window of cognition
it blazes ! illusion chases illusion on speed
there are big streets and hills to climb
ear fills with ovations in a foreign language
insect empires thrill in an afternoon heat-wave
corn lies down and people talk about futures

trade and investment and cheating for money
and love the transgressed are the transgressors
to write a poem ! to forget how to speak
and the discourse on the properties of Delta
statues line up for the Latin lesson for grass
to grieve for the dolorous elements of marble
I am Anchises ! I coupled with Venus and knew
darkness to be the crown of deceit passing
before the eyes twenty four chapters including
the one about the Cyclops and rocks tossed
into the waters—how many times ?

09-07-21

ET EGO IN ARCADIA

they give gilded acanthus and crowns
incense tumblers gypsum and ivory effigies
all to no avail still the nymphs weep ceaselessly
and goats clamber gnawing on dry rock
the heavens are not heard ! how many Aprils
in any given year ? the word is out—
ships will not sail seas grown dry climates
of fire drought and city-destroying floods
lurks a demon in every household darken
the larders empty baskets of dust and
insects for Apollo has turned his back
King-of-Mice keeps his distance in remote
caverns steep slopes that look out on
the other worlds weight increases and depth
none who step out can recall the way back
bickering and envy replace the court-house
cannons are devised and oils that defy water
bury the head in stone and appeal to archaic
deities gone blind and dressed in birch-bark
fauns and centaurs dance with stolen maids
it is not music ! raucous noise decibels
of violence and lust drum and broken chord
sits on temple ruins Orpheus bawling his

eyes out and wherever one looks clouds filled
with lice and locusts swarm the horizons
so none can plant and reap harvests and bitter
acrimony instead of love the hastening trumpet
cracked lips of war resound even as the Pest
runs its maniac strides through hut and hovel
palace and mansion strife and rumor !
you think these are days of progress ?
inventions of keyboards and electricity only
give rise to deviance and mendacity
mind is a sieve where stolen identities flourish
and masks copies of personas who never lived
and shadow and corruption and Money !
new ways of writing wax clay and papyrus
to record falsified accounts ledgers ciphers
where are the naked followers of Pythagoras
and from the mystic orient voices of *denial*
■■
retribution and repercussion talk of the Soul
the Mysteries ! who are the Few ?
the wish to be Whole ! *circles* ! Ideas !

09-07-21

ROCK FRAGMENTS

and after all that fails and light diminished
by so many disappearances inexplicable grief
shorelines sandy mounts hill-dialects on the wane
nothing left to interpret let alone to reclaim
life as it was somewhere between fading grass
and the rock fragments littering the park
formerly a suburb of paradise forlorn and
characterized by betrayal of script and sound
a reckoning of sleep and its antagonisms reading
from right to left before the hair-line and midnight
alone and with sorrow if one could have some of it
back if water in the ear tremendous seas roiling
wake to the nightmare clatter of hooves striking
against the glass or rain inside the theater

whatever eclipses reason or grammar and what
is left what remains of the great story and its
fleets and rioting hemispheres of lunacy and
nation-states aborted in their first naval battle
schemes and ideas the *mind* effervescent ploy
gift of the gods counting the days before
the prediction comes true the absences the clones
in the mirror copies of actors without pronouns
which is you which is me the fright-wig and
Cassandra on the top step a can of malt-liquor
in her left hand a piece of rope in the right darkening
stagecraft of illusion enormous segments of history
to be memorized and the children too in their
scuttlebutt and nuisance making sounds echoes
of the first life the one before birth this one or
that aping ministers of war bards and mountebanks
who can recite at length the Rg Veda and to what
avail this dictionary of claustrophobia and aphasia
find ourselves bereft of routine on the sidelines
puzzled that the world has gone by without us
just these rock fragments and cave entrances
wild memories of youth sawing away at language
discarded elocution for babble and barking
like hoarse Hecuba at the moon's fading homophone
to remember ! but what ?

09-08-21

THE COSMIC MYSTERY

"Scylla latus dextrum, laevum inrequieta Charybdis"
                    Ovid, Metamorphosis, XIII,730

ninety and a half by the hundreds falling
out of the clear blue and making cities where they land
infested dangers menacing renewals of thunder
flint and brimstone sparks and ashes incendiary
deities the size of ants swarming abandoned planets
what distances and longing what on-going alphabets
the world is somewhere in this chaos talking Mexican

erecting geometrical structures the size of India
where a Buddha is born one of five trillion ideas !
such is shape and gravity culmination of waters
everywhere an equation that brings to life a ninth
grade Latin class and suddenly effigies of teen-agers
flooding the marble lobby of the Mayo Clinic and Lo !
staggering from an athletic bout the god Neptune
for a drink ! acclaimed and carried on their shoulders
to a football field and left to meditate between goal posts
I was there ! but when I cannot recall a lonesome
moment in the edifice of existence and others with colors
and bandanas and head-strips and jimmy-tools all
running wildly mostly in the southern direction
where fealty to the dead is great and jungles and
hidden plateaus and Brazils or the Deccan fetid and dark
lift their topographies fruit trees banyans banana plots
coconut and maize and fantastic temples multiplied
with more than ten thousand cosmic deities coupling
in stone and gravel copper-hued or tawny like lion-manes
what does it matter ? the Buddha-type looming in his shadow
of grace and entelechy and the Librarian ! codes and
skills to read and the aggravation of colonies and uprisings
here it was a strap for the hangman and there an Asterisk !
so much to learn and just as quickly unlearn in life
the years revolve evolve and disappear leaving a detritus
of posters and peeling murals walls surrounding Troy
in all its decades phantomatic and pornographic Helen
reviving herself in the pages of a Grammar text all riot
and suburban in her under-hose the legend reads a Mystery
can we ever understand ? lessons from the Ramayana
flying monkeys and ten-headed Demons and maybe Vishnu
it is too much there are not enough numbers and the Buddha-one
in his variety of sculpture and dentistry and the Soul
left to shift for itself between the many lotus ponds
of description and tattle blue bright red fuschia and *amarillo*
hues and deserts and finally mountains moving slowly
across the western screen to escape ! which Buddha is it ?

09-08-21

WHAT DOES IT MATTER ?

the dread and longing the fulsome shining
mysterious apparitions walking planet sleep
before one knows waking is over and dense
and depths the cavernous and lacunae mind
its own *selva oscura* the wandering head in
downstream evocations glimpse on either bank
the side of time that has no memory brother
and grass folded neatly together reunion
of the soul with its long lost and houses upon
houses going up and down darker avenues
trees are possible for ascension and skies just
known through a manual on pronunciation
right thinking the virtues keys to Beyond
if one could apprehend the twilight blossoms
sun's waning echoes stay in a motel seashore
Scylla named for her neon and tress and comb
the entire display of one's breath the coming
and going the eventuality of another encounter
spirit world daft projections of vowels south
leaning against a trunk blasted oriental with
budding ideas the thought to exit this cosmos
for what ? remember the time on the slope
noon verdure kids shouting vocables a pure
noise mythic and oracular to listen carefully
and *know* ! this is it their flaring wardrobe and
cosmetics and dangerous at once the realization
charades and shadow-play and puppetry copies
of childhood and grief as always the consequence
desire after birth and among such others to speak
saying nothing the usual hand-shake goodbye
to the earth seeking tumulus and detritus Latin
poetry in long unscripted nonsense found in a
bottle floating in the green scum pond lotus
shaking its hair out in the southern seas reddish
kaleidoscope of entries retroflex and vivid
as nights can be on the sought after coasts where
occasion and circumstance among leaves and
vie for form the slow spreading ink of oblivion

09-09-21

AN ELEGANT NOISE
for Max

when I saw angel scatter-shot fall from the heavens
nine times I counted the solar homophone
nine times more I heard from afar the longing cry
flame and bursting acetylene lives of the Caesars
and aerial artists dangling by their own saliva
more than nine the cipher that equals eternity
by a half and nothing more but the susurration
of the Stygian waters and the ear with its decks
of lookout and escape and still kept falling angel
more beautiful more lustrous than sandalwood
or moon and everything is repeated in the trumpet's
muted wail we come and go fly and fail splashing
into the inner drum and loud and instantaneous
the duplicating asterisks of angel's distant jazz
the antique ! sun becomes so hot it self-incinerates !
wing and tip and flash of time outside of number
space before space the engines of grief ignite
what is it to read the texts of either margin ?
caught falling like a frail shadow the soul's angel
asleep within the sleep of eons the eye alone awake
watching the cosmos wage war against itself
diamond versus ether in a blaze of sound and metal
bright ! echoes of galaxies in repercussion and birth
I know you ! in a trice you've come and gone
a blast of mercury a poisoned hemisphere of love
chances of recognition like vapors in a southern wind
the dead ! you foremost among those wayward beings
listing in sultry channels timber and rotted planks
detritus of the human condition hanging on but not
hanging on loosely afloat drowning in oxygen !
what machine can extrapolate your essence from
the wreck and dismemberment of mind and age ?
your hips your knees nine times I re-counted them
lapses and hiatus immersion in the nine atmospheres
noise of derailed trains of burning coaches of alcohol
derangement of progress in its futile disregard
for the antinomies and vagrancies of life on earth
you were one ! you were butterfly and hummingbird

113

dust weighted your wings a solitary jewel faded
as you sang those coruscating final notes and *Bang !*
when angel finally hit it was in the rust of memory

09-10-21

NINE ELEVEN

one brief moment of illumination
with incredible speed gravity and motion
everything takes place battles earthquakes
oceans capsized mountains writing is invented
rocks lava sands gravel Mind of all things
happens and poetry and monsters and gods
and lovers and texts of unbearable sublimity
takes place the instant a body occurs it dies
sweet and bitter seasons change roles rains
meteors and the Mahabharata and silk sashes
neckties and drought poverty above all and
cheap politics long droning sequences of verse
Chinese tones Greek accents folly and rancor
envy of the immortals jealousy of borders
immigrants and chasms the number Three !
between you and me the fast and elusive
passage tickets trains airplane rides sleep
waking in unknown locales space and motels
keys lost divans and rigor mortis bee swarms
metaphysics and used clothing the need to be
the inability to understand the children who
lose identity masks and fiction and unfinished
paintings everything in a single instant from
the beginning of geological time to the end
of space the dark immobility which is a seizure
the random excess which is breath Memory
the mirror suspended between past and present
figures and obligations repercussions divorce
singularity illusion of the unending and grief
mendicants and investors lies deceit surplus
war after war plunder greed mercy at a standstill

pornography and ego restless dream-sweats
it goes on and on the frivolous furtive fugue
assuming there is a point myth and substance
logic ! fingers lost in grass waning sunsets
hill dialects recognition and amnesia longing
forgetting the room number being alone
the denied self the purge and exile forests
inextricable mazes wandering without thread
it ends it all ends in less than a minute
planetary errors galactic rumors of extinction
the time you and I met we grew suddenly old
windows relentless silence leaves darkening
light dovetailed in itself and stone and weight
were we ever young before we turned to statues
frozen in that moment of illumination ?

09-11-21

AENEAS OF DIDO MOURNED

the famous inch of light fabled and lost
grimoire and fuse of a riddled memory
places called by their inhabitants for burning
loosely collided seas for another yearning
to reach shores sandy banks cliffs transformed
with human names tendered accounts false skies
lakes too where plunge feet of shadows hissing
with regard to the east and pluriform deities
snakes crocodiles massive rutting elephants
some speaking loud as statues turned to cinder
by noontime's civil war cannon as others stop
difficulty of retracing pauses and hiatus linger
hands that clasp while a section at a time simply
falls away leaving sky more opaque the bleak
afternoon when childhood ended toys littered
shop doors burst open lurking deaths from before
and metal still too hot and stories their innocent eyes
listening when the profound noise from nowhere
and gather some similes a metaphor and aphasia

myth of language talking sleep the distances !
it will be hazel-wood twigs and twitches the spark
of amnesia folded inwards the eyelid at levels
too secret for hearing even as sight the vision
repels the oncoming fortune of breath too late
we circumnavigate the hope of an alternate Africa
exchanging signals red and blue the fragments
that never cease falling into the waters below
I am without a pronoun and you coming closer
we recognize the shape but not the outline
placing head to stone and stone to speechless leaf
coordinates for a voyage without return

09-12-21

TWO POEMS : AN ANTERIOR LIFE

i

the words at first half-sounds echoes
of previous lives resounding in the ear's
phonetic ruins a salt-shape a cairn or
tumulus of archaic noise fictions and
fragments of wind and shadow leaf-
torment aphasia that counts among
the dead the least distortions of water
waves that plunge the sleeper like a tree
into an anterior existence in search of
an exit into the accident of light outside
the hive of memory and loss distances
and bedsides the fever trembling in its
shimmering mercury attached to a brow
antique as stone and gravity the longing
for weight and height and resonances
hum and buzz that conform to a rumor
of air incidental as a labyrinth in July
the focus of grass on the dusk when
fingers are likely to detach and vanish
days ! who can account for their number
equalities of metaphor and signal ringing

against the metal of the numeral Three
shorn of sense the passage through matter
insect kingdoms composed of pure heat
reddening and dialects where hills monitor
meaning falling asleep in a picture book
depicting the innocence of gravel the voice
of the wheel directing night into chaos

ii

and see no more the sun's new bright nor
by night the wheeling galaxies and asterisks
punctuations between lives the nominal
absence of breath left to tarry among cliff
and mound whispering litanies of grass
sealed off from the following day and here
and there a window and lantern signals
from afar that is no more the legendary
pronoun nor sacked cities on the margins
ant-hills dispositions of amnesia and mounds
there to wander bereft of memory the slope
and dew-line the syntax of leaves the augur's
moment to speak in trance guiding the sky
above to plunge into waters of beyond that
are as persons talking in an immemorial sleep
the self and its shadow mask and rope tossed
in the aerial act of oblivion repose and shift
come to a standstill trying to remember and
only *that* before the great yawning hiatus
that separates immortals from the dustbin of
history the smaller effects of thought and
myth arrangements of sound and denial
loss! not to recognize *the other* but dismiss
from the hour the relics of conversation
waking but not awake in the wood where
copies of light lend to the maze an accidental
impression of living moving between Helen
and Osiris a hand a nod the eye's remote
flicker struggling to recall who the image
in the mirror is smoking and disappearing

09-13-21

TOUCHED BY CIRCE

haploid exit to the past a rumor
seconded by windy threats from Circe
lowing and disease in the leaf mourning
silence in Diana's woody realm
duplicate of en error in numbering
the foliage verdure and blowsy autumn skies
animals ! in each other's eyes we fall
embracing shadows and effigies written
on the walls of distance and aching
to know who we used to be and who
we really are pronominal suffixes to texts
of vanishing futility the forgotten diphthong
in a school-boy grammar an erased idea
passed on to the girl in the back row
a date on Friday night with a *beast* !
from what oriental birth story do we arise ?
talking to phantoms from a decimal system
who bear news of the next existence
in their tormented gazes and we turn
to the second floor for a game of charades
transforming and being transformed masks
and object lessons in disunity and from
above a celestial hand descends groping
bodies are only simulations of attitude !
like stones falling from a passing planet
we drop into sleep's drugged labyrinth
dreams ! Circe daughter-of-the-Sun
touches each of us with her wand
treachery and deceit of earthly life
the gift of light ! as if waking from a coma
we search on all fours words that never come
hebetic and aphasic our mute selves
loss and eternal longing

09-14-21

ECLOGUE

what is the preterit form of water
realm of the naiads the undulating
face and distortion depths where
light is a filmy ghost and the fishes
of the fathers electric and dominant
lurk in stone and abusive algae
names that waver between sense
and sound echoing vast and remote
as if sleep within sleep unfolding
diameters of a new distance liquid
and draining from the ear of Dionysus
rivers ! *Nar* and *Farfarus* winding through
the poem about Diana and the mortal
chase and day's unfocused drone and
bees bordering the hem like mists
alert and dangerous making air unfit
to breathe stifling dense afternoons
when persons exchange beings beside
banks of reed and sedge and the pipe
with its single note of destiny high
and inaudible & then shepherds tumble
drowning in embrace of nymph and
caryatid becoming reliefs in marble
that fingers read in the archaic fuse
of trembling lamentation and leaf

09-14-21

MAX : A SECRET HISTORY
for Marilla

a sad thing it is a while ago like forty
years compressed to the size of a thumbnail
was it the fever or something else the sound
of metal in sunshine moving like a street
month of May that never concluded unless
time is different in a coma the sweet end
darkness involving darkness the self denied

windows don't matter but exhaust fumes
clouds of envy yellowing in the thick before
you know it another century a bridge of
shining over an unseen river or a travelogue
to the distance of someone else's mind
cannot get over so many the hours of motor
and sky evenly distributed in a small reverie
dreaming it isn't so nor ever was a birth
going in circles the x-ray and isotope both
on a hill the other side of which is a dialect
in a language without vowels like the Himalayas
burdened with the Buddha's *dusky* jewel
going slowly down you can see three thousand
feet the bus held together by rubber bands
and rhymes asleep with the tiny dignity of
insects ripening in corn fields south where
the dead multiply their silent fracas a loud
longing shaking slightly in the leaves out back

09-15-21

Mi hermana : Cōātlīcue

unconscious dialect of the cordilleras
that lie south of the great world cemetery
just off the carretera Panamericana
mi hermana who is synonymous with
Mexican independence a fiesta in dusk
and the remaining light that cascades
over Lomas Chapultepec is today ten
less than a century a perennial flower
who came to the light in our geminated birth
juguetes ! toys presented in her 7th year
dressed me up as *china poblana* frowning
in dusty Aztec photographs loud with
mid-20th century communism and art
so much language of horn and tribulation
floating gardens Xochimilco and telegrams
reporting avuncular deaths and up and

down the steps on Calle Tula how much !
hanging clothes on rooftops and sun and
constancy of the sun's marvelous homophone
speaking only Mexican and driving a lamp
into the hemisphere that exists between
the pyramids of Sun and Moon and more !
she is my memory of a world full of *tios*
and *tias* and *abuelos* all with surnames
of distance conquistadores and mestizos
did our twin shadows eclipse her ? she
who was more mother than our mother
a refuge and a discipline to exist despite
disharmony and alcohol and tuberculosis
early years of darkness frontier crossings
playing with sidewalks in LA train-rides
to impossible hills where snow and ice
speak riddles to skies of cold opprobrium
bobby-soxer ! Ink Spots and Frank Sinatra
and Nat King Cole beside Trio Los Pancho
"To you my heart cries out Perfidia!"
back and forth from basement to attic
and back down again to a hell of *otherness*
wet-backs all but orphans in a Lutheran north
lipstick was sin and hiding phonograph disks
and learning to be defiant through heart-break
what was her early marriage to me but sadness ?
her absence only meant I inherited her room
with its slanted roof and star-filled window
how many nights endured with mystery
finding solace in her various new dwellings
on the Mississippi or by lake Minnetonka
and grown up and six children and like a saint
denying her comforts for others and living
gospel humility always on the fringes of
a society menacing for its post-modernity
but for me her *Juanito* and even more so today
a lifeline a voice to my own puzzling past
three thousand miles away she dares to
celebrate 90 years on September 16th
el Grito de Dolores ! fiesta and tapatío !

mi hermana Laurita !

(Coatlicue, wife of Mixcōhuātl, also known as Tēteoh īnnān, is the Aztec goddess who gave birth to the moon, stars, and Huītzilōpōchtli, the god of the sun and war.)

09-15-21

CHAOS !

great the silent seas that flood the ear
falling from one sleep into the last of many
paradise of gravel ! wheels that never turn
stopping by the mill-pond cruising dark
the lonesome detours and forgotten hills
where uncounted days lie abandoned and
the shifting night slowly erases its galaxies
portents of times to come ! hands unfold
documents of aerial ignorance and fingers
of their own explore the wayward grasses
where memories of cloud and afternoons
of eternal heat linger and shadows concur
in finding bodies structures of wind and leaf
things without assembly matters too broad
to imagine distance can exist and how to
wake and perceive the sun's holy homophone
a dereliction of mind assuming pronouns
are destiny and that light will hold sway
in a numerical promise of heaven even as
avenues tree-laden with shade lengthen hours
and it is *us* becoming watching and waiting
for the map to deliver its cities from order
into the chaos of childhood with its asterisks
and bottomless waters and the swirl of noise
and hue the very dimensions without measure
we are the horizon ! pitch-black the thought
of immortality the threadbare nuisance of
matter and flight the libraries ! it is always
the same day no difference no change slight

nuances of memory the dilapidated automobile
motor still running and the ditch by the side
where Greek kids named Ajax or Diomedes
spin tales luring words from their shape and
sound and nothing is pronounced correctly
and high and remotely loud the finishing touch
to the poem without meaning syllable by
unuttered syllable bottled in the Sibyl's mind

09-16-21

THE LOST SOUND OF MEMORY

the fall from heaven with a favorite knife
to severe light from the hand it shapes
the mechanic and the angel with Etruscan
wings half above earth and half buried in
a terra-cotta urn and when the peacocks
start the dance and a recitation drones far
to the west of Siam whose mountain is reduced
to a small illegible inscription on palm-leaf
instructions pausing to sleep and start
the ignition that sets darkness into motion
immense phonetic decay that defines the ear
cloud-physics in the movie theater sorrow
implicit any given afternoon come sundown
lesions and metaphors for skin and death
hold on ! the amphetamine of doubt stirring
in the body's phantom other half a cup
for the oracle and diminishment of thumb
ocher hills of dialect and ambush flickering
that sparks a dialogue between rock and
stone intense and poignant silence of leaves
how much otherness can a morgue survive
in the narrow continuum of space and denial
whatever repercussion echoes in the furnace
or in the glass emptied of its illusions is small
by comparison with the hallucinatory memory
of life's imminent shipwreck and language

as many alphas that dot the brain's frail
encounter with waking and disorder loud
the vowels scattered across a single lunation
& consonants rattling in grief's dusky bowl
a single direction *south* province of the dead
and gods in disarray one floor up from earth
waters and indignation surmounting night's
distant houses with their stucco and ivy and
anticipation of avenues staccato with aphasia
dark lawns resonant with noise and breath
tiny illuminations of insects and galaxies
all in one instantaneous frame of existence
once big and bright now meaningless *sound*

09-17-21

THE FUTILITY

Max! come look at my new book—
it's not *The Invention of Spain*
but something called *The Blank Page*
and that's what it is a blank page
because you are not where you should be
Joe! where in the universe are you?
I need your address so I can send you
my new book—it's not *Comedy , Divine , The*
but *The Blank Page* and that's what is
a blank page because I can't find you anywhere
trivial joys being human a success *here*
to counter the many failures *there*
autocracy versus democracy sheep in
wolves' clothing the lesions of conspiracy
and doubt and poetry in the midst
of this ungovernable psychotic world
a single finger lifted to the twilight
and then lost in the roaming unmapped grasses
childhood reverted to its own adulthood
the fierce rejoinder of silence to language
nonsense and rumor the ultimate error

of thought and bankrupt illusions of mind
detritus of the temple ruin by the roadside
pray for us Minerva ! for what ?
one more opus in the magma of letters
a sliver of light among empires of dust
and orthographic missteps and the whole
teetering chronology of literary histories
a footnote at a time and to remember the meaning
of grief and longing loss and sorrow
the multiple inventions of Agamemnon or
Achilles weaving duplicitous shadows on a stage
or crazed *apsarases* drinking oil in their lust
we are here for less than a flash of a second
loud and cheering then suddenly on our knees
bereft of cognition memory an afterthought
write wrote written ! for whom if not for
the dead in their tiny cathedrals of snow and dew
but if they have forgotten how to read ?

09-18-21

THE INCOMPLETE TITLE

is it any better in Hindi than in Spanish ?
glory to the scribes of poesy who dwell
in wind-castles two flights up from the Port
devolving and rotating repetitions of sounds
the dog is a text and its memory is a river
that is a duplicate of the long forgotten when
parks and trees that dwell in night's swarming
details of insect phyla brought us no closer
to understanding than the clinic and its marble
lobby clamoring with resonance and reflection
invalids chaste and whispering in operatic Italian
warning signals fobs broken perfumes opium
the lesser part of childhood in fear of *knowing*
until grief the sleep of centuries the head-sets
apart from stone like a cyclic friction sparked
at the moment of death regarding to the far left

a position once occupied by smoke now a letter
that can never be written correctly the rumor
and abatement of space ! in search of a new
vocabulary where a mailbox ceases fitting
outside is everything skin and desire the song
a repercussion of anomie and forget-me-nots
please be my own ! vertebrate splendor rose
and eye-shade serpentine quiz of elephants
just like the verses of enhancement and doubt
overloaded baroque ether in spirals of psi and
incubated in the mind's fertile and knotted chaos
to look askance and people the parenthesis with
asterisks and bees setting aflame the empyrean
and nothing more a conjecture of air as if
there could be no other autumn the land astride
burnt three times over the clusters of azure
and mutilated stairwells meant for cigarettes
the ever-world of poetry misfired embolism and
dialect continuum in sequences of fiery red
someone in the rear of the envelope shouting
to be left alone ! *memory* astray in its inks
and alabaster summation of noisy time
but no peace at all for the book !

09-19-21

A DESTROYED WORK

flitting and transient the airs of the sky
vocabularies rhyme-schemes metaphors
and plagiarized epic battle scenes aflame
man's lot ! an eye on the traveling cloud
on bees and distance itself a bluish haze
dying in the moment letting go of fingers
that still clutch grass and the mechanics
of noise figures and shapes of heat
drill and dark opprobrium of memory
stunned as it struggles on the broken
step with literatures in half-spoken

tongues bric-a-brac and irregularities
winds that snatch whole trees at a glance
chimerical load of a cathedral's weight
on the tottering shoulder to the left
errors of a rumored month given over to
a banished coral-reef's hues and colors
grammatical iridescence of the galaxies
wheeling through an evanescent syntax
man's miserable lot ! misunderstanding
and ambulances and no-exit signs in red
dialects that encumber twilight hills
islands of asterisk and hyphen listing
below the meridian where the dead vanish
with their imperishable final thoughts
breath the Logos and immortality !
signals from failed angels seraphim too loud
for ideologies that circle uselessly
the crematoria of philological antiquity
man's undressed lot ! relatives and unknown lovers
mourning on remote afternoons the tumulus
of a pronoun that lacks vowels and punctuation
hiatus and decibel of the copied metronome
that accompanies the plunging planet Ivory
blood that saturates hotels with weddings
poets and scavengers millipedes of Spain
the song at last that is never heard
guitar and spleen and alcoholic fame
continent of Japan drowned in liquid opium
the longing and futility of the leaf

09-20-21

ANOTHER DESTROYED WORK

what is it at the top of the stairs
that is so frightening ?
copies and metaphors of a previous life
or merely the ghosts of cigarettes and
contraband verses cribbed from Ovid

translations of air ! situations no child
had ever imagined rotating around a noise
heard just once in the middle of the final sleep
to never wake from *that !* the various and
plural mystery of a misunderstood word
judgment and hiatus of the day that never comes
a symposium of afternoons on the banks of the *Cocytus*
intimations of the *other* dwelling secretly
in the attic where model airplanes
devastate memory with their mission to duplicate
and pausing before taking that last step up
to the top where darkness holds the knees hostage
and night-spells and the virginity of smoke
to begin to write ! inescapable clauses about
immortality and the fane of Diana after school
and the metamorphosis of football heroes
into pigs and salamanders and virtuosity
of a violin string performing the Spheres
to grow up one day despite the stairway
and fear and osmosis of the light that penetrates
without illuminating folding over and over
the paper with its initial poem and antiquity
blossoms borne by Zephyrus and the claudication
of voices trapped inside coral and ivy
redundancies everywhere ! we have lived !
enough and it is the hour when the head
turns to stone and the great chronologies
of trilobite and minotaur are laid to rest
somewhere below the bottom step
in a riot of silence and defused ears

09-21-21

MAX THE ARHAT*

the star ! the one unaccompanied by cart
or steed the shining blasted through its skin
later a legend in distant asterisks the panoply
of sounds and vertigo leading to the street
how can we ever apologize to the dead
for our constant error ? a breath a rock
gravel and discolored grass evening's
tremendous rumor of darkness and finitude
language does nothing to correct the misused
pronoun the sibilant discord the nuanced letter
shaking just above the neon where everything
is repeated and yet nothing is recognized
we run through lives like water our legs fold
our knees plead our shoulders mourn losses
that lack definition there are immensities of air
clouds like raffia shredding in the bower of sleep
the star ! remember when he was born circling
around his novel brightness and vowels
cadenced and shaped like immersions of memory
and hands and the effort to walk without help
wheels and foreboding and the entelechy of combs
everything is divided by three and hemispheres
integrate their darker halves with oblivion
destiny is a mirage shaped by fingers of shadow
however much regret lays hold of our gypsies
walls ferment and riddle the mind's waking state
hasps and conjectures and sails torn apart by
the gods in their stormy bickering over death
the last minute is the first one of eternity !
they stare with amaze at the invention of breath
speed and gravity and the forsaken conjecture
the star ! unable to sustain air and its satellites
the world an on-and-off switch that ceased working
the night when rain created its own forty year cycle
fever and its multiples charts and faulty radiology
the intensity of the single and irreversible cosmos
deranged and plummeting into its own lavas
punctuations and the ultimatum of the hiatus
levels of despair and silence of the archaic leaf

40,000 *arhats* carved out of teakwood suspended
in midair between justice and compassion !

   * *an arhat or arahant is one who has gained*
     insight into the true nature of existence

09-22-21

ARIOSTO
   "con tal rumor di timpani e di trombe,
    che tutto'l mondo par che ne rimbombe"
       Orlando Furioso, XVIII, 41

fourfold the archaic convention of sound
minutiae of air fascicules of cloud *the orient !*
and they say there is no number greater than three
the fixed fire in the eye ! the dragon and its letter
trees that grow downward to parody the Acheron
virtuosities of elimination by noise the roundelay
and its discipline twice told by nightfall and those
gathered by the hair and cast out of the city !
cascades of a single vowel ululating and Angelica
gorgeous in her flaming Hollywood wig the lure
canned laughter and holocaust of the insect world
champions on black metal steeds racing blood
and impropriety the fashion of love the elixir
troubadours and Dante and the famous Saracens
blotted skies naked groves flourishing with nymph
and acolyte and the readers of pornography
the Parisian exiles Charlemagne the arch-demon
the flower-of-Spain ! caught in the defiles of passion
all guitar and hair-pomade and Valentino-eyes
dark sparkle the platter of renown and madness
who can extricate Moor from Florentine in battle ?
it's a high-school skit drugged and frilled in finery
of Byzantine excess and the neighing and whoa
bickering dallying on footfalls and tender ears
why is it taking so long for photography to develop ?
fly me to the moon ! doomed anchors in dust seas
Renaissance capsules to whiten and deny *pentimento*

for every cathedral a thumb of suspicion and Ho
neighbors and strangers and beautiful witnesses
scavengers of language the retreat from sound !
fragrances drifting from the imprisoned syllable
surprise and omega the catastrophe of learning
there is no part that belongs to the *Whole* merely
the abscess of philology hum and drone vocabulary
of arrows in flight or cudgels and iron bats spare
no brains the hills and lacustrine vergers green
even as twilight's stained ocher emerges like a film
exposing to the light the multiple struggles of dark
versus enchanted palaces princesses missing combs
and head-ornaments the pearl and nadir of despair
sobbing into the paraffin of entelechy the depths
is there anyone in poetry who knows how to ?
Berlitz sessions with Lorenzo in the Aula Magna
new fly-fields paved near Ancona and off to Mars
to break the net and set Lady Venus free ! aloft
with Astolfo and memory of the myrmidons for
this is epic stuff the wagers between vernacular
and the classic Eight small grammars and texts
recited by the henna-painted houris of Zaragoza
it remains for the hidden lake the submerged city
the necropolis of Pluto the causeways and firms
of a duplicated imperial Rome and the warrior
caste itself to complete these seditious octaves
imitation consonants ! repercussion of the horn
that Roland blew at Roncesvalles and shot
his temples out with blood so clear and bright

09-23-21

OTHER PEOPLE'S HOUSES

it's not the grammar that's different
we is they even on the radio a distributed noise
singing parallel lives we can little know better
ours being as indistinct as theirs sleeping
and kept to the self even the pronoun has trouble
a revelation of otherness in a crowd of beings
such as one door can never open while the next
is hard to shut looking out on the gravel
the keen awareness of painted rock and stone
a garage is darker than most a car moves
only at night gleaming hard like a god in distress
hearing about their dreams are ours the worse
and ringing the bell on any pretext just to look
inside what a vast room darkening in the corners
if only a window with curtains from Asia and
who's to know where the voice is archaic and
too soft to read a newspaper by the exits
not clearly marked and notice the carpeting
worn maroon or mauve or hear a hummingbird
as if trapped in the basement stairwell how it got
there is a divination and contexts between planets
theirs being the hard bright knobby thing circling sleep
contests for light and breath are their children
really better at anything the lawns are a crib
for insect realms and listening close to the soil
the ear becomes profound lost in a labyrinth
of tongues working to be understood however
expensive the lessons are a longing to overcome
to get to the other side the backyard the slopes
that converge on the orient of all places big
with a volume in gold-letter head stolen from
the library despite the paint dashed on its green cover
when they got married and how many their offspring
we us them theirs why if ever tangled shifts
from blue to red litmus indicating dates important
for their anniversaries blowing out candles
and darkness not intermittent but permanent

09-24-21

THE SUMMATION

repetitions as they grow fainter and copies
and duplicates of eroded memories of sea-
and landscapes of the puzzling mind abscesses
of thought a portfolio of lists incomplete and
illegible as the reverie and phantom of love
backyards and fading photographs of sounds
meaning truncated at the wrist and knees
rendered numb by amnesia and disillusion
the pain of shoulders at the wheel and driven
syllables and equations that numbers cannot
count the zero and its horizon the distance
of the rose from its seed logic and illogic
the hap of capsized norms the plate-glass
windows used for suicide shattered noises
that cripple the ear and white nights on end
the round of gravity and its homophones
exclusion of final consonants and such as
they are the vowels on their string of smoke
wherever we are the mortal din compounds
confusion and lunation of missing months
the forgery of twenty-eight harrowing days
guided by the sun's blackened hive of flame
sulfur and retrograde motion repentant aleph
postponed omega the excuses of an afternoon
spent in alcohol and darkness the embrace of
a divorcee in mirrors cracked by bad poetry
whatever goads the mountain to its accolades
and hills that grow dense with dialects spurned
by lamps and acetylene and diesels that round
hair-pin curves only to plunge like planets
into the waters of the Lethe and so much else
envelopes filled with hair and caution and flight
of the transient soul burdened with insect guilt
and pleading on the altar of repercussions
the plaintive mortal bereft of medicine and gods
to die alone ! thread that lacks its labyrinth
fuse and thrust of breath all too brief
the hand and its multiples spanning thin air
in a cathedral of vanishing leaf and silence
was life ever otherwise ?

09-25-21

PYTHAGORAS

"Omnia mutantur, nihil interit"
Ovid, Metamorphosis, XV, 165

recognized the shield the painted tears
and cracked greaves the fallen sighs and
bridges between head and mind I saw at once
the transformations from man to beast and
the soul fluttering centimeters from the pale
eyes both shut and wide opened forever
on the small scrutiny of sky where heavens
disappear to make way for the sequence of hells
the bottomless water beneath which the great
fire burns taking boat and wind to final ashes
and heard near and far cries of mothers
from children rent and grammarians blinded
by the Rule and sophists on their knees
gibbering as bats in a mutilated cave
waxen figurines lapis lazuli and gold ingots
tossed into the ditch and ornaments
of cities too immense to describe in orients
of language and decay and augur and haruspex
speaking like mirrors in emblazoned noons
their brains transparent as insect wings
predicting the end of time and creatures foul
and fair fleeing the inch of pitch and sulfur
about to fill the vacancies of space
and the constant reincarnations of matter
sentient or immobile the planets with identities
struggling to return from birth and the fading moons
like goddesses bereft of knees and wit and
the earths minute and wobbling without consonants
the tragedies written in the other hemisphere
and the outcomes of man like a vehicle of the Unknown
both horse and rider interchanged and sight
and hearing and the blossoms that astonish
on the Wheel's charging rim and yet
failed to recognize any more who I had become
all flow and image and the dust that gathers
in the dialects of the western hills
to seize with hands of air the *thing* that flies

imperishable and unseen leaving behind
the noise of words the rumor and error
between deaths of illusory pronouns and births
that repeat uncounted cycles passing through
the sun's archaic and inconstant homophone

09-26-21

METEMPSYCHOSIS

that flies in figures invisible brief
the experience as light is the fiction
roaming between atmospheres of noise
and error I was a peacock and then
darkness of winged night to recall
otherwise the day came and went like
a statue of silence was dancing mottled
earth a space for a moment phased and
argent as the moon in its vowel of height
could dizzying apparitions and planets
the size of asterisks the parallel life
of insects in the field doubling song
in issues of heat and mirage of highways
to the east and mountains that lift
and wander the world like women
in search of their deity in straps and
cosmetics the ruffled waves that come
running to greet and glistening distance
deaths and hills buried with cries solo
voices imprinted on the horizon's echo
to finger the remaining grass an hour
before disappearance of the solar orb
a consonant that cannot end pronounced
dusk even as vague we limit the sound
and hearing listen for the walls to emit
secrets spoken into ears of stone the
rumor of gravel and wheels coming
home

09-27-21

THE ENIGMATIC DAY

nor is there color left to the sky
Lucifer exits and to Phoebus pass the lamp
did from windows derive etymologies
guesses that linger in vanishing dew
identities sparkling in the hummingbird's eye
dissonance of the orient in grammars of
ruin and rumor the smaller mounds the dun
and ocher that field their distances
just by waking and spread awnings of caprice
and longing over newly minted lawns
wonder that to walk and spend what
are hours like days trading voices with
shadows at play with images of time
find and lose at once the moment of eternity
half in the air and half darkened gone
around the sudden wall and was not there
before and missing links between sounds
fingers that elaborate vowels and leaves
winnowing from the clouds a dactyl
of despair and hoist the ear to the branch
aching to hold the wind a minute more
sprays of light and humid relics of noise
far and farther yet a childhood without memory
will lay to rest the donkey of humility
and spare the death mewing in the eaves
how ! it cries and weeps the monogram
stained against the stucco's briefest touch
plum blossoms land without gravity
and one and two the mortals that mark
and end their nativity in grief

09-27-21

THE RUMOR OF LIGHT / THE ERROR OF BEING

what does it mean a Baedeker to the coasts
where the black boats are beached and phantoms
none have survived the voyage across the waters
just acrimony and doubt the fierce quarreling
spates over a girl cross-eyed with black tresses
furtive indignation an image that excludes vowels
lessons never learned sea-tumult and mutiny
will the Trojans never understand the brevity
of it all the inconsistency of spears and oaths
the gods what are they but knots on a rope that
cannot be untied and stone and the grievous sense
locked in marble the hewn epithets of sorrowing
mothers and the cages suspended where gibbering
imitations of heroes molting like birds demand
back the shape of their shadows the wary rumor
of the soul's incessant passing from birth to birth
forms and migrations of tongue and fossil the width
of space contained in the small green bottle that
none can reach and to no avail the multiplied verses
and the hexagon and the cross-roads with its ritual

to return one day as persons or masks of right thinking
with respect for nature and the mountains that bore us
to the sun's rising apophony and the small memories
that define us whittling our timber and notching
the air with excess sounds the verbiage of cloister
and madness and the recognitions abjured and faulty
one against one and the number three that reflects
a stubborn desire to count the makeshift stairs that
lead toward the symposium of signs that infect
the night-skies with astrologies and theogonies
literatures ! noise of plot and meter and longing
what is it we identify falling asleep ?
a hand dissolving in its own design—

09-28-21

THE INDISTINCT CONFINES

rumors of afternoons that never come
and steps half built that aim for the heavens
and smoke and incense and turbulent winds
storms that writhe within a thimble's size
the worlds and their evoked excess of dark
heaving breaths the contours divided between
the first and second numbers revolving white
into gravity and space the incandescent vowel
and fulminating final consonant and who
can emerge from dreams a different soul a mask
petrified by the moon's reverse and asterisks
that burn forever in the punctuation of time
hours like silhouettes of excised hands and grasses
that strangle twilight at its birth the anomie
and reduction of life on earth the splendid
and coruscating palaces of light but abscesses
and errors of a divine conspiracy to halve
the universe into unequal remnants of eternity
what's to be born if not to die in the shell ?
murmurs and whispers among the talking leaves
and statues that ignite when the sun's axle
is at its height and steeds of black sweat and
promises of infinite days when memory is no more
but sands and waters lingering on imperfect shores
the voice that was the child the fiercely ringing
note that spends its labyrinth in the mortal ear
to dream of *others* ! the pendulum of oblivion
that swings from birth to birth faint shadows
that pass from becoming into being countless times
the mind and its foreclosure ! blind seers counting
islands and sharing a single rotation of thought
cliffs ! the abyss whence all things arise and return
sleep the enormous and blank continent
that consumes the indistinct confines of distance
beyond which *nothing* establishes its echo

09-29-21

138

THIS ORPHIC MADNESS

memory is a circle and meteors only
strike at age thirteen when Eurydice
unattended arrives on the inconstant shores
a crow flies east towards manicomio
and autumn's varicolored tempest the mind
arouses to duplicitous reveries of love
a child a boy a girl a skirted wind in hues
of radiant but tarnished gold the oblivion
promised to mortals sweeter than the forbidden
fruit the apple in the bird's-eye of death
and follows streams of vagaries perfumed
nights under a canopy of fireflies the lies
and tongues of absence and unseen orients
rock and stone aflame with secret passions
the grass underfoot the gravel that wheels betray
the lonesome windows that flare up odd hours
in motels on the brink of emptiness what
do they contain but chambers of temptation
delusional fabric of breath and vistas
just outside the common route of corn-fields
and insectaries empires of heat and bliss
stolen everything the kisses sealed by sun's
enormous homophone of noon and sudden
winter's frozen metals and lips of unspoken snow
how unyielding the sex of time the furious advance
of age measured in the inch of a dozen years
before occlusion and repercussion take their toll
embraced in the swart glance of deviant gods
bee-swarms that advertise the following model
amorous crescents that blaze like honey
shimmering in the air of trance and asterisk
a death ! announcements on parchment
of disappearing ink and who can ever
pursue such noise the Spanish folly
of a music bidden to enrage the torpid clouds
that muster their regiments in eternal dark
the rivers that march with fluid feet
and on high the celestial instant with its sound
that goes round and round in a silent math

the pyramids ! the song and stark obsessions
decades are but an instant in the dance !

09-30-21

THE HIDDEN SUMMER

Mr Chin on his death bed answered that
he was memorizing the words of the Buddha
in the same hospital another former employee
the librarian in infatuated with Michael Jackson
was recalling Purcell's chorus *A boozy short leave*
before yielding her ghost to the strains
of Bach's Toccata and fugue in D minor
a gifted organist herself now a phonetic decay
and on the very same day on a sunny afternoon
July 3rd 2006 a Sunday my brother and I
embraced parting forever on an empty corner
in San Francisco a minute of multiple forebodings
the deaths imminent from the moment of birth
the concrete sky the horizonless event
the moments that are so final yet of no surprise
the consequence of *coming-to-be*
desires wants passions signals missed in the grasses
that flood evening with regret and longing
a practical course based on graded reading
Beginning Sanskrit years in the offing and
the distances of water and the hills that outline
an east that cannot be encompassed let alone
recorded and the slattern lanes of Chinatown
not far from Jack Kerouac alley
everything embroidered in the slight sweat
that graced the upper lip of a lover waiting
in sumptuous red-ink calligraphy one
who had given the self over to cancer
sometime in the eighties of the last century
so much ! time is a confused mechanics
a brooding unconstructed syllabary of sounds
and repercussions anachronous and violent

the future being a constant seed in the sun's
black ovum the rapid fire insurgency of the
Unexpected like faded saffron photographs that
spill out of order on a lost backyard
in Brooklyn before the invention of the internet
waste ! denigration of the perfect vowel !
there we were once a blind zygote about to split
now a pair of wayward aging punctuation marks
each going his own way into eternity

09-30-21

SELF-DEFINITION

not words but lunar cavities the dark light
that illumines the cosmos while I sleep
to come to terms with myth and noise
the sections that have been removed from
time the disorganization of vowels and syntax
the ruin of sound as it reverberates in the ear
of one who has just died or am I that one being
and nothing more passing through volumes
of unwritten text the disjunct consonant of
sorrow as it refracts in the long afternoon of water
a discharge of pyramids and their fossil hummingbirds
to catch just a wing of childhood the butterflies
and flutes that summon hills from their depths
of dialect and resonance I am at a second remove
and distill memory in a phonetic cacophony
that only tears can clarify the subjective looming
in the mirror's septic quadrant and what is
the background other than crepuscular voices
taking shape between branch and ogive I am a planet
a mooring on the space of echoes where distance
gathers its skirts of dimension and gravity
to plunge ! how many are the masks of night
the terminus it is being a man the horse and
its plenitude the *sun !* suchness the whither of fate
dice cast hands removed feet at a loss as to knees

the antinomy of recognition in the drug that
takes the skin from its body and sets it moving
that's me too the abracadabra of a grammar
in fields of heat and passion the framework
of a single homophone representing first love
the dynamic of hair and thistles and combs
everywhere there is a *face* ! but when the news
arrives that it has died passing on to a sphere
where leaves and silence surrender their domain
then I am a spirit too a transient whim of cognition
somewhere in the envelope of transformations
an etched asterisk endowed with speech a motion
taking place on a lawn in 1956 and loud and high
the bright texture of summer air the immensity
reading between the lines the fall of Troy

10-01-21

THE TRANSCENDENT MOMENT

and all that follows the ignition of memory
what abyss and what cliffs ! the horse in its diameter
of heat and yearning placed in the midst of a yard
and to marble turned in the noon episode of challenge
and response the seed of origination blackening
in thought and deed exactly like the poem recited
in the afternoon's preterit tense and from on high
the god of reckless intuition begins the phonetic destruction
of language with all its flaws and faults the bric-a-brac
of reason ruined by its own anticipation and the sound
imminent and casual of adolescents bickering in corridors
at length with the repercussion of hills and accidents
where the highway's asphalt intersects with breath
what ! blood and its mythology and theosophy spent
in a measure of hours that last a single minute the glass
and pyres of illusion that we have mattered naught
in the consequence and drivel of the daily debate
this is yours that one's mine even as the motor flies
out of control the throttle and brake at odds with light

registers of vowels recorded out of context the enormous
epiphany of cognition between lunations the vagrant
and casual symbolism wagered in a flower-bed
that drifts on the opposite shore ! out of reach the hand
declares its own dialectic and goes lost ruminating
in the tremendous grasses of night the tender and
innocent moment of recognition dissolved no sooner
is it perceived and punctuated by space that travels
at speeds incommensurate with the recollections
that the past devours in an enigmatic play-script
rehearsed by children who have just woken up
in the ripple and ebb of anachronistic rivers
running soundlessly below earth's chaotic surface
we are there drowning with echoes and masks
unedited pronouns fluctuations of meter and voice
end-all of transcription and bone-text copies
nothing but copies of an unremembered life

10-02-21

VARIATION ON A LINE OF ARIOSTO
"E sí tre volte e piú l'ira il sospinse"
Orlando Furioso, xviii, 23

then but what silence translated into integers
silver assonant effigies hypnotized in aerial
turbulence a dialect apart from the whole
a stigma to sound essences issuing like gasoline
sieves and coordinates seas rushing wild flues
consonants abandoned in moon-tide slow flux
earthly wraiths ghosted plying cloud-looms of
grassy depths darkening homophones the glint
trembling on the echo's ridge noise and tumulus
pronominal deaths uncountable surplus fiction
rue and fuse ignition's memory densities grave
fixed in polar seclusions the sun's enormous
error already too high to match as plungers
flame the steeds in their swart indignation sent
pitching through paper zodiacs thrust and drum

repercussion of illusion's bedside story-telling
a finger a watch a glass-eye a framed mirror in
quicklime the despondent planet mercury seized
and spent in ambulance graced with foliage even
as speed lessens its gravity entering a second child
the resemblance to the former the cataclysm of
thoughts colliding with metal reverberations and
asterisks ascendant in order of sleep and entelechy
a poem preterit afterlife in unfound words still
and the patient in his unit trembling to utter
just one of the syllables attributed to marble
and fawning and great lawns of evening alcohol
at last reunites cognition with its own oblivion

10-03-21

DISCOVERY OF THE PAST

para mi Hermana

was in the basement where no natural light
filtered into the dank recess obliterated by
piles of coal and the odor of urine in excess
wooden structure sagging would it ever fail ?
tiny white flowers in a world all their own
growing in a long narrow swath just outside
to the east of the kingdom until then rooms
in irregular sequences governed by heat and
the water pump which despite all often froze
could discern little of the books behind glass
or the lugubrious tap-tapping of marbles
taking small leaps on a perforated board
colored to resemble China at its apex with
imaginary rills and rock-sites and dandelions
in profusion at the bottom of brown paper bags
corrosion of distance the dun and ocher
metaphors of ancestry whose hair filled
small ivory boxes or sealed envelopes hidden
carefully behind the Emperor's two-way mirror
if time were static and gravity the labyrinth

of flight then the attic's mysterious summer
would extend into the minute eternity of
the flying insects that clamored for success
in their struggle with death and its shapeless
demons whose laced embroidery disguised
the false opulence of sitting-room furniture
an enigmatic radio claimed it was always Sunday
a periphery of incomprehensible voices making
noise and clatter of talking symbols prepared
to walk out of their phonetic frame and strut
sticking tongues out shaking hips and singing
songs imported from a Broadway somewhere
in the far orient of the country of our exile
was it the mourning dove in eaves of snow
reminding of an abandoned solar paradise
and the dark repercussion of a train-ride
through the unending mountain of night ?
the beginning or the end of a parallel life
tear-drops and tulips and celestial rumors
resonating in a garage ignited by alcohol
and the oracular white whet-stone with pedals
one for each foot of the Prussian Colossus
who collected insurance on accidental days
country saloons barber-shops fishing poles
left to idle in lakes that forage on clouds
numinous with Aztec pyramid recollections
the Past ! did it start when we fell asleep
falling off the moving rail-cars into the clinic
where they x-rayed our bodies and gave us
futile grammars lesson in dusky red brick ?
fusion of lament and sermon sanitariums
remote passages to colonies of sorrow and
winters the length of an afternoon in black ice
slow re-entry of light seeping through clothes
hung out to stiffen in below zero weather
a face a finger a blade of grass an evening
lights on and off strangers for Sunday dinner
and absences incomplete and troubling as
the terrific ticking of the ornate time-piece
that dominated the tar-dense atmosphere

and always night that brought stairways &
sleep in the incremental inch of the Past
and sleep in the incremental inch of the Past

10-04-21

LIVES OF BROKEN CIRCULARITY
for Max

lives of broken circularity ours the wind-span
of an echo vertigo and black-glass prisms
can no longer see as before the legendary graces
mountain and integer of space the reckoning
at home nowhere with pages to go before the end
in clauses of retribution and cancellation the light !
descending from preterit skies the few memories
that count the opaque days with skeletal hours
advance of noise in the shell where former seas
renew their absences and where is the armor
donned by errors in grammatical form a statue
to dissuade the union of atmospheres tragedy
and repercussion of clouds high in the mind's
attic the airlines that rumor guides toward letters
unformed in the chrysalis of doubt we are in that
divided wheel going forth and beckon to hands
from their aerial transformation a semblance
of childhood the backyard an evening darkening
of missing voices and grass the token greenery
of sleep lasting until the signal and catastrophe
small and unprepared at first the casual sore in
the mouth the trigeminal nerve the loss of function
pervades the word reducing it to its original sound
the logic of assonance in the recital somewhere deep
in the auditorium of longing to recognize and yet
not perceive shapes issuing from grief the agony
and trial of mortality in its inescapable misstep
breath ! released from the circle of no return

10-05-21

FLOW MY TEARS

the sheer and inactive the indissoluble and final
burning the heart's immobility to ache thrust
pursuing phantom regards the lessened hope
a first and a last beside inert the bundles of cloth
tatters and rags to weep for the foregone concluding
treaties streets and asphalt walking bruised the winds
assail targets blown from paradise here unto shores
they haul the black keels up and offer prayers for
a reward of breath the extra day all wish for but
denial and repercussion the slamming drum clouds
the other side of the wall if to hear and could it be
there is no alternative to the revolving door chaste
and startled the nymph who governs the opposite shore
waters no matter and the smaller grasses the yearning
indecisive animals at the foot of the famous oracular
tree branching towards remote sounds the meaning
and the incomprehensible called language provoked
a text writ large on the verso of air as it suspends
in the homophone of light its own sun the noon and
spent cannons and lawns that go lost moving west
efforts to describe but fail the vowels of intent are
only a mystery to recall the clinic's granite exterior
opening brass portals the statues ruminating in the
polished lobby recriminations of life-support systems
the doppelganger effect charges the atmospheres with
bolts and threads like missives or metaphors of blaze
inserted the dream a still-life painting showing paths
windows out of which falls the bride and flow my tears
each is the severed hand of memory the deconstructed
portions of an inscription no museum can offer to read
without grief the gravity it instills the sleeper endows
depths of leaf and dew if only the margins keep
and yet give way to undersides where Persephone
holds little sway and count the darkness everlasting

10-06-21

ASK AND ASK AGAIN

what are the gods but obstacles ? litigations
between light and breath the invisible script
that governs mortal fates the dissent of tongues
and the wary hills where dialects die all to the gods
attributed and why pray and sacrifice to these
entities obese with unearned glories like stars
mutilated by desire and perpetuating false glares
are you and I intimidated by their promises of death
eternal as the instant of oblivion ? search as we might
in texts of archaic enigmas & broken rules of grammar
vowels out of context and the jungle of consonants
meant to sound and echo things posited in higher
spheres a music not meant for ears and a shining
destined for other eyes than ours legendary spots
bright and ephemeral numbers that pepper the skies
with asterisks and smoking embers astrological
zoologies and theogonies of brief mentation
a whole without its parts ! what a cryptic debacle
the immense conflagration of learning ! pronouns
without substance wayward masks caught in
an ungovernable dance you and I missing letters
captured in a net of grass and leaf children forever
lost in the immemorial moment of recognition
and consequence playthings of illusion and harvest
one by one the summers we thought eternal fail
in their capacity to extend heat and the apiaries
that lull us to siestas of make-believe and *what !*
the gods the long and unwritten narratives of
their great escapes and futile bargains to cheat
and delude while shimmering on the rim of space
yet planets do proceed to their own extinctions
regardless of the foible and repercussion of myth
buried in libraries where they remain unfinished
booklets you and I continue to read in spasms
of punctuation and oracular unconsciousness
when were we ever really alive ? ask and ask again

10-07-21

EVERYBODY'S IN THE DREAM OF DEATH

not just number two or three nor the Greek boy next door
who was dragged by a trucker around the sun's orbit
and never came home to rest the underside of grass the great
tomb of air the fastened and the unchained syllables that
the winds hollow out of the sea's myriad countenances
hard by the well or next to the crumbling garden wall
intimacies of insect grammar the teratology of language
whether sung by the bard of the stricken hiatus or spoken
by the rhetor of broken finger-nails the text the dream
the vast orient of sleep the lapse into a fault-line dividing
the immense southland of the dead from the hemispheres
where dwell the bed-ridden the despondent the nerve-spent
those who house cathedrals in their aortas and those
for whom the only direction is north/northwest and spirits
and anemones and winged illustrations of distance and
finally the consonants that characterize planets as they plunge
into a meridian of dandelions and bird-song *how much !*
each is an every of another who has lost hands sleeping
in the ditch of bottomless sand the failed bargain of breath
satellites in the flickering neon announcement of tragedy
and thence the plethora and tintinnabulation of noises
tiny syllogisms echoing in the flooded ear of Stone :
death is the volcano and its fireflies of memory
death is the intellect in the migraine of Minerva
death is the chisel of Juno's immortal envy
death is the Grand Canyon simply put
death is the Grand Canyon and *all* Natural Wonders
death is the annex to the Mayo Clinic
death is the snowstorm the day the Twins came to daylight
death is the brother who came to understand the other side of time
death is Mary Lou Willard baring her soul in a corn-field
death is never the next time but in shortness of breath
death is the Enchanted Island where men become swine
death is the imperfection in literature to say anything clearly
death is not the cremated one but the *witnesses*
death is the playing field where kids chase an elusive ball
death is the gasoline pump and the radio and the pearl necklace
nothing else matters in the dance but the partner who is death
death is the twenty-five cent chapbook sold on the corner
death is pencil and paper and astrolabe to show the way
death is the lucid moment of eternity when the child *forgets*

and in a brilliant flash of silence everything ends
death *is* the dream a corpse is having about the inhabitants of light
all else is sundered from the norm of thought
death is justice meted out in a Chicago movie theater
death is the wedding party and the summer vacation
death is the map of the swimming pool
death is death is death is death is *the* orient
death and only death is the heart *and* sex of the Beloved !

10-08-21

DEATH IS THE PERSONIFICATION OF IDEAS
for James Balfour

the irrelevant field of development and technology
just when the asterisk intersects with the hiatus
studying at this late date the Symposium of Plato
do you remember how it was on the blustery corner
where the Mayo Clinic erected its granite stylus
high into the frozen Ojibway heavens ?
A-B-C you don't know what you mean to me
the indentation where I waited for your car to pick me up
what day of the week was that I often transfigure
these memories into a study hall the length of a cigarette
or find myself with book in hand just wandering
in a traffic of heat transfer and idolatry of women
soon it will be the day that comes around with its dead child
the fuming hour of steam and heraldry
on the way to the library to look for the *Loom of Language*
so many impediments to right thinking !
the how and the why of the simple vowel on the street
when no one is looking and skirts fly into legend
the ear with its obstacle to grammar
and the eye cyclopean and loud !
there were days on end when we just did not *know*
and suggestions to travel south to climb pyramids
to exchange hands with the border-guards
things you could recite in your sleep with fireflies
listening to the screen door slam unexpectedly
or the mysterious world of gravel in darkest night

separation was a terrible thing to learn
first it was tuberculosis then going to a summer camp
that excluded you and writing letters for the first time
longing and the incense of passion in an envelope
what would you grow up to be ? a social worker ?
watching the trees exercise their memories
sometimes no more than an hour long and summer
the asphalt paving and the decisions of grass to idle
in quick succession gods came and went with syntax
and hieratic rules of pronunciation on graduation day
the rest was down-hill missing slopes and dying
trying to remember between courses in cloud physics
and entomology the way the world was directed
funneled into a Sanskrit ideology of sound and deafness
the discourse of religions ! always a matter of leaf
and burrow and meditation in a retroflex consonant
the harmonies of past existences and the cheap
derivations of desire and fear in this one
sail on little Honey-Bee !

10-08-21

DEATH THE SIZE OF ITS OWN ETYMOLOGY

we were driving around in the old powder-blue Pontiac
with a radio buzzing songs from the lunatic ward upstairs
the drink went a long way to dousing our rationale for being
and sudden as a trunk in the middle of the fork we exited
a surmise that pieces of the sky just might be available
in the underbrush where the small dappled deer of memory
graze and after that what more can we say that hasn't
been reported in clauses of indirect speech the liturgical
tongue of statues and cannons even as the court-house
celebrates a century of living rock and diameters of light
fell the inconstancy of shadows walking on amazed pavement
imitating the voices of adolescent girls whose enormous chatter
elevates to the empyrean notions of thought and asterisks
loneliness and attitudes of mechanical forgery of pronouns
will you be me ever more ? it asks in a forensic dialect

of hills and abundance once more we try using Spanish
for its oregano and pimento and yet nostalgia cannot
still the anxiety and fervid sense of speaking to no one
as the highway offers detours to cities and landscapes ignored
by the painters of the high school arts class and Look !
a red-winged hawk takes to the heavens making loops and
short circuits in the already electricized air and we stare
becoming eternal in that off-moment of ecstasy and oblivion

10-08-21

LA MUERTE EN LA CARRETERA PANAMERICANA

who steps over the crimson line
and who holds back from the escape
or adventure of breath the lingering
effect of a mind troubled by its mirror-image
the toxicology report and its afflicted aftermath
assigned to a belief system that includes language
and speech acts the marmoreal role of statues
in progress and long noontimes spent in the beatitudes
of adolescent love and thunder storms
as for the madness and kaleidoscope of poetry
the event horizon of the incomplete verse
or the distich of unremembered syllables
nothing is forever and lies and transgressions of color
hills of forged hues and dialects the omission
of consequences the brilliant array of skies
the Buick traveling through dust of ages
to its residency on the black island of Venus
belt and radiation copies of human error
the effort to sidestep and conform to mortality
egress of waters the darker swirls and swills
where hell-demons spate over the corollaries
of judgment and wrath the impossibilities of Dawn
breaking through the sound-barrier of sleep
how many horses must we ride ? the corrupt
and inane steeds swart and nevertheless divine
emptiness at last in their wake hullabaloo

and imitation of shadows cast against stucco
and the tobacco leaf and its partner the empyrean
immense travesties of existence and its asterisks
the uncountable oracle the strait-jacket
infirmity of thought the famous pearl-tight
imperfection of dreams and on and on
a hand struggling to resume its waking shape
and fingers without which grass lacks definition
and ever the pyramid and its brother the isosceles triangle
brooding like Aztec homophones atop
the rusted metal vowels of the conquistadores
darkness punctuated by motels where *death*
high on amphetamines and turquoise
hallucinates about the life Beyond

10-09-21

DEATH IS THE MUSIC OF THE FORBIDDEN CITY
for Rafael Jesús González

I salute the great half of the sun that still remembers
and as for implacable night a gesture of primroses and gravel
the crummy fatal interstices where boys become men
the summers fleeting though myriad that pass through the eye
into the depths of pre-birth and oblivion where hands are
nothing but an iteration of the desire to become conscious
and fingers the flotilla of grasses that whisper vanishing
into the twilight hills of memory and then only sound remains
the melancholy echo of stone residing in the ear's tomb
if anything had to be memorized it was the indelible script
of light wavering like dew in the morning of the dandelion
a traffic of insensate vowels wheels of wind and cloud inane
proclivities of gravity bringing planets to their dusty knees
what seemed to be transactions between mortal and god were
but dreams of speech and hearing immemorial crevices
in the rock fragments of cognition and noon the statuary
of motion and grief and finally the nothingness at all of
coming-to-be and to walk and reply to shadows of glass and
leaf the very monuments of unlearning and saddled to steeds

plunging through the abscess of dawn and what a holocaust !
bright red the film and reverie of inspiration which is only death
wearing its beautiful mask of plumes and silver-work and
whatever follows is a pursuit of mirrors through the backland
the floating gardens of childhood and the very mountain
erected for the moment only to teach about the skies and
autumns that do not come and go but remain as symbols
of falling and descent into the uncountable cosmic hells
one after the other placed like a broken ladder beneath
and forever earth's fragile homophone the other half
of the sun blackening in the inconstancy of time itself

10-10-21

DEATH IS STILL IN HIGH SCHOOL
WAITING TO GRADUATE
   for Bob Ness and Slade Schuster

the Greeks were first and still are in riot
and seclusion of ideas and circulation of air
unraveling clouds skyscrapers have yet to touch
however much the class draws its curtains
on the second act and the girls in frizz and jet
ready their hair for the prom and what a night
metal the size of moonbeams and forest murmurs
crickets escaped from summer cornfields
make serenade between the walls and floors and coke
and the boys tight in their hoodlum best array
necktie and pink starched shirt already drunk
half-pints of cheap vodka or a shot of brandy chaser
the margins recede and Latin exfoliates its grammar
no one listens to Caesar's sheet of irregular verbs
it's all Etruscan haruspex in a bottle and the Sibyl
of longing in her evaporating evening gown a voice
between syllables mysterious enunciations of rose
and garter the high fix of combs and eau de cologne
on their wrists the goddesses whose faces are mirrors
and an orchestra culminates its drum against
the valedictorian's speech act such as statues are

and the candid appeal to the heavens of the Druids
stalking woods trees with memories of the year before
when the highway took its accident to Troy and loud
and tragic the recital of lost names the reversion
to type wearing mask and persona the pronouns
of the second person deleted the honorific Spanish
introduced just as the slipper falls from the prom-queen's
left foot or it is rigor mortis the horror of it all
in a restaurant operated by the Myceneans poison
is diluted in the fancy wines and the guests totter
from dream to dream before forgetting all about life
the horns are outside and belong to automobiles
and distance slowly takes its hills away
night is no longer sudden but a breathless punctuation
the ampersands and asterisks begin to burn
someone to the far left of the class photo
begins the long interruption of language accentuating
the beautiful and gorgeous denunciations of echo
soon time will be on the other side of the drug
and few will recall who the stranger was that
came to take their shadows away one by one

10-11-21

I AM NOT THE SAME AS THE OTHER

when it comes around in the end you have become
a riddle of memory situations and side-stitching
the ego of once before a reduction in light
hard to differentiate the principle of isolation
from the dictum of make-believe it ever happened
as it is the phone rings only to warn
before hanging up and stare as you might into
the grammar of the night skies which have been
a long time in appearing it is all a mirage not
a miracle a fiction of identities using voices
to deny the self immodest and mendacious
you consider turning the ignition off even
as the four-wheel drive verges toward the cliff

it is only a copy of something that never occurred
a fragment of rock set aside for analysis and
the suture slowly unravels over the wound
which is grief continuous and bipartite
to sleep would be better an office of dreams
usually in a cave with reason and intoxication
how much day seems a relief until the second hour
passes and illumination is seen for what it is
a short-life battery unable to resuscitate the child
who has just entered into a durable coma
summer after summer and suddenly it is penance
the freighted instant when eternity turns into
monotony the trembling homophone of the sun
shock still above high noon and the horses from
somewhere come into the yard magnificent
but illusory a moment of disregard and routine
resumes its appalling distances in Sanskrit
which is waiting for the Chinese translation
the exegesis of *Nibbana* while the rest of you
the divided and inexplicable personae of your brain
simply resort to the river-bank to graze
you set your head to rest not on the stone
but its shadow and what is to know ?
the unspeakable text of air remains as
mysterious as when you were born
and you fumble trying to read the leaves
and watch the small dappled deer come
to nibble the grass beside you
you are one of them

10-11-21

DEATH IS THE ALLEGORY OF LOVE

cloud stuff not gold plated earthling dimmed
with seizures and desires to overcome dust
the particular sky that resonates in dreams
that sleep is not the only reality but
a facsimile a copy or forgery of another life

the breath that sustains the poetry that lies
the drug required to see straight the essence
like peninsulas of gasoline and ether extending
into galactic portals where the other sits waiting
to look back at you the animal of effervescence
quizzical enigmatic erroneous wandering
what's to know you ask repeatedly to a drum
that resounds in a labyrinth of air the smashed
receptacle of hearing the tiny dots of light
like flares to measure distance slowly going out
were you there ? at birth a prominent asterisk
only to fail in prediction and repercussion
alone and with grief the victim of a sun-spot
a whorl that invades thought with rumors
of what lies beyond around you the passengers
in their mistaken best peering out windows
that move through and between the mountains
collapsible heights stricken planets plummeting
behind the ear and to appear knowledgeable
who is speaking to you in a pre-literate tongue
a half-formed statue a hemisphere of cognition
doubt that south is a direction the incidence
of coming-to-be denied in court as the cannons
fire another salvo at the descending gravity
do you land both feet first ? the existence of time
divided into monopolies of days named after
celestial deities pornographers witless gods
is yet to be proven even as you walk the sundered
plains the drought and emotion of mortality
what a promise ! keepers of the secret doors
hold everything back you knock and rustle
the mattress springs the brain detached from
the semaphores that keep bedlam at bay
and you resurface somehow cleansed but
not purified the holy steps to take to ascend
the ladder of illusion smoking as ever that last
cigarette struggling to recall the face of your
first love the sheer and shimmering mirage
combs and earrings small tokens glittering
her eyes the dense pools where you drown
embraced and absolved in oblivion

10-12-21

DEATH IS THE CLASS VALEDICTORIAN
(for Thomas Lake, MD)

sterling of character gifted with syllables
knew where to put the tonic accent and
how to wield the circumflex in seasons of despair
draped the statue with emerald gravity and
spoke as if the world were a small gem whirling
inside the tiger's gaze no stranger to untruths
selected for his hair pomade and the color of
his east European eyes that gazed forthright
into the vacuums of almighty space a thought !
unbeknownst to him winter had already mantled
his human torso with a defiant grip no words
could undertake nor was he conscious of going
naked like the Jains avoiding any step that would
annihilate whole insect kingdoms but went on
with his voice of echoless sounds a brilliant array
of augury and despond the meanderings of a
pronoun too proud to understand and forth
he went silver-tongued and brittle all firm
with a college diploma already in hand and
degrees in infinite medicine tools to undermine
Persephone's little plot and Lo! did he not see
Pluto standing near ? but like a calm insouciant
Jesus kept interpolating right syntax between
the plunging planets until the end of his discourse
found him applause and one-way tickets to Chicago
the thunderous ovation of paper Jupiters and
the headband worn by Minerva in childbirth
dead already from the first utterance of glory
dead from the start in his two piece suit and tie
dead because he could not hear music blooming
in the plum garlands worn around his neck and
especially dead simply because of the anonymity
he had to share with everyone else just born
a hypothesis of intelligence a trouser leg rolled
halfway to the knee a purloined shoulder and hands
that could not sleep for grieving the human mind
death took credit for his stage presence for his
aplomb and lack of poetry for his ordinary

misunderstanding of *das Ding an sich* and
outright for his polished foot-ware unwavering
even as fell forty floors and twice as many years
to the starry absences of all forlorn mankind

10-13-21

INTRODUCTION ALLEGRO AND VARIATIONS

"Lastly, and perhaps most importantly, we can no
longer speak with any sort of knowledge or confidence
as to how — or even whether — the universe itself began."—Ethan Siegel

and death was the hidden
motivation
of all poetry
and gravity hidden
inside death's cold footprint
was ever the withheld breath
innocent as stone
underneath the head
that sleeps

and when the Buddha was born the austerities
the Vedic rites the canopy and the white parasol
astonishment that it will take so long to graduate
and formalize wandering forth the brick and grass
to lie there face down in the refuse victim of the sun
deny the antecedent and its eternity all things flow
to read as if with understanding the text of tears
and with sorrow give the hand its due and let go
the mendicant from his illusion the day-long math
of undivided zeroes and echo from afar the longing
mountain and pool that reflects nothing back but
chasms the mind the orphaned soul the unwitting
animal pondering its nativity among herons and
scorpions a lasting shot from the hunter's bow
the gateway to heaven it's called the suburban car
the antelope and verdigris of discontent how far
thought can travel from its corpse

it will be a form of language hewn marble
the pedestal and grace to resemble air and
nothing else invisible architecture of sound
inching out from the assembly of clouds
ravenous to devour time's preterit sky
the little wisps and tufts that madden bees
and disorient the envelopes of stolen hair
when was the last one born and which is
the twin of his forged pronoun the blackening
wick of torment and solar epiphany the loud
witness to the start of the next eternity ?

words have no logic to be other than repercussion
echo of dissent the ricocheting valleys of the ear
dun and distant the reverse of mirrors darkening
in a version of night imperfect for its asterisks
and half-shaped planets the homes and future
of liberated souls whose faint imprint and type
are the haunted dust of butterflies the fleeing
hiss of shadows longing to be grass again

all poetry is naught at its origins
a space to fill with sleep and sand
small figures rounding the edge of light
flames and phantoms yearning for circularity
the bottomless sea the very noise
at the beginning of the cosmos
or the infinity that precedes that
endless beginning

the young priest was here yesterday
the gardener asking about
the strength of light the wind
blossoms pink and variegated
falling from above
to the depths below
unseen and lost
this life
was

10-14-21

DVOŘÁK'S SYMPHONY *FROM THE NEW WORLD*

the dehiscent sky in translation a distance
more remote than the ear's enigmatic silence
the avenues repeat themselves tree and shadow
slowly becoming a hill a height the allegory and
metaphor of life before air the illusory syllogism
I know you were there too and the fox and the aerial
creature the dragonfly hovering inches above the river
did we wait it out ? the sequence of memories broken
in half by what we thought was the engine that supplies
the wind with bees and the literatures of schoolyards
empty but for the dust and cracked concrete a shell
hollowed out to capture the riot of afternoon voices
captain of a squad that tosses the ball back and forth
you hesitated before deciding there was music but
inaudible the leaves the insects teeming in their industries
of dirt and semaphore what else we wended our way back
across the highway where the Greeks got killed by diesels
and found evening less roseate amorphous and anxious
yes the windows inking over with mystery a hand all
but invisible beckoning to futures without grammar
simple sense of clouds shifting their continents of
dead gods even further from the edge of light where
night waits to manifest a sound issuing eerily from
an unidentifiable rumor perhaps the thing caught
in the wire-mesh fencing around the swimming pool
we guessed that the maps we had drawn that day were
already archaic with their confusion of language and
clinic the glass metabolism the books out of reach
the histories ! on the bluffs mentioned in the symphony
buffalo shadowy and proud with their herds of natives
disappearing from the text just the flinty tips of their spears
still glowing like fossil stars in the fabric of death
the undeniable

10-14-21

DEATH IS A LOVE SONG

what finery is this double-shine
this array and splendor of sun's outlasting rays
this dizzy yet solemn instant craved by none
yet spent in finitude of love ?
songs that spell the constant eternity
of a fleeting kiss the blown-away lyrics
the fireflies and the clarion call of the screen
afternoons spent in the length of air
that swirls around the evidence of time
languid postures cornfields distances beyond
no eye can climb depictions of syllables like
mountains pronounced in silent rhyme
the whole which is half its parts declared the soul
to be a circle of divided skies a murmur
of clouds the shape of echo and myths
of noise that engender photographic reveries
girls whose sudden appearance on the upper rung
of the ladder that only goes half-way *there*
lipstick and combs and perfumes in tiny vials
symbols of heaven's remote realms
dreams and sleep and tombs lined unconsciously
on by-ways and margins and rivers that split
into a thousand mouths deltas of dark swooning
acres outside the city walls dedicated to the Muse
a chant a relic of Egyptian harmony sistras
and tambourines and henna-designed palms
the script of notes that evaporate and the index
of fingers that go unraveling the grassy scheme
death is a wonder the chorus of repeated verse
to live and love forever and a day and yet
to fall the thousand years it took to see the light
and gain for nothing the sealed envelope of night

10-15-21

SIDDHARTHA

is this the epic about old-age ?
what about the women in their fine jewelry
hair-pieces combs ankle-bells all coming apart
jostling and clambering at the top floor windows
or even on the roof tops clumsy sleepy-eyed
just to get one last look at the crown prince of Youth
straddling by in a sumptuous gold chariot
drawn by four of the best caparisoned horses sleek
and swart as if compelled by a god with banners
aflutter and half-moons in the sky a dozen at least
the blue-lotus-eyed fawn in his soft armor of summer
a length away from distance and resembling nothing
less than the mountain of reveries azure and dusky
in the twilight of time and the echoes and noise of silver
bracelets a-jangle and the whimpering sighing cries
of the women high above the city elbows and hips
out of joint their breasts heaving with love and longing
passions ! the blaze and asymmetry of adolescence
out of proportion to the drug that speeds through the veins
blood is at a premium and oils and pomades and lip-gloss
the throat yearns to be more than throat
and shoulders vie with knees for supple motility
is gravity the enemy ? from out of the limpid infinity
of sky stretched to its limits a bull of thunder roars
hailstones the size of Crete the maze and whirling
instruments tuned up to deafen the incessantly craving
god of the underworld Yama wanting to outdo in beauty
the stunned Siddhartha slowly circling on earth's rim
will he too grow infirm and dim of sight ? Charioteer !
turns the steeds around and heads back to the palace
away from these hovels of charity and the loud waxing
sounds and turbulence of the mob-voice and the women !
above in their unthrottled license and ambiguity
eyes bedimmed with blackener and tears and hands
losing grip and the painted fans and invitations to the dance
fall like so much confetti to the royal thoroughfare
the epic of old-age the void and repercussion of absence
the stuttering and stammering the halting step
the stone ! the head worn thin by the lice of indolence

and desire faltering unable to hear what follows silence
the universe of mortals pock-marked and jaded
to sleep again in the Garden never to be born again !

10-16-21

RIDDLE ME THIS
"Por que é que ver é uma tal desorganização?"
Clarice Lispector, A Paixão Segundo G.H.

beware of gestures the hidden speech of statues
do not misinterpret the flights of birds whose
song is in the ear the distances that cannot ply
air's loom the fraught winds of nocturnal tempest
overreaching waves the somber reflections seem
to rise against tides that swallow shore and cliff
steep lies the dark and depths unveiled by heat
do summers cross your path and autumns sadden
and brides have lost their way and the hills of
dun and argent reveries why go on the road is
hard and has no direction and in their intermittent
guile the gods have fashioned you like me to puzzle
why forever more the seen is just illusory the felt
a mask of dissolving pronouns the heard is but
a drunken note played across a broken reed and
what do others seem to be but a crowd of shades
waiting on the river-bank for the ferry boat
to bear them to some remote dream and as for
you and me why does a blade of grass separate
our memories from letters of a forgotten alphabet ?

10-17-21

A CONUNDRUM

when in my clouds I cease to roll and listen
to the thunders and swift lightning bolts
cast asunder my former skies and sleeping
in rushes and dark loam I take my *sigmas*
and my *taus* threading ancient stone with
mindful knots and prepare the fall to pass
through uncounted gravity and spaces too wide
to bear and through unnumbered lives am
reborn and born again to fail arriving at noon
with its syllabic horse and heat of statues and
the cannon whose aim is justice at the bar
to imitate the breath that was and copy from
a relief in living rock the outlines of a life
and consequences of my last death like swirling
bands of honey-bees that assail my thought
some metaphor this is a simile or a circumflex
the furious doubt of my mind to design its fate
or my body still walking down the royal path
to encounter its double in the sparkling dew
the drink and tomb of reason the shelves aloft
that glow like stairways leading to heaven's
false gate to turrets and high-walled citadels
a populace of insect and apiary or the small
deer that pause before draining the pool dry
countless times this moment has been eternalized
repeated and sent on the shuttle back and forth
a repercussion of memories and x-rays silent
as the bottom of outer space faint shimmer
of the eons that went before echo of an echo
plangent planets that grieve plunging destinies
comets like children in language's enigmatic
sounds the noises of splashing rills or crevices
where death's fingers play the endless rote and
wheel that none perceive though tossed senselessly
in its forever circling gyres and never come to rest
motionless yet unceasing in constant rotation
the moving shadows that blacken sun's violent
homophones in the mirror-play of time
yet that cannot end what never was begun

10-17-21

DEATH IS THE AUTOMATIC WRITING IN THE AIR

the free verse of yesterday a cosmic reality
lawns and strophes of irregularity and grief
which was the last to be seen and the first to go
beneath the wheels of the racing diesel motor
a Greek it was foremost among the missing
hilt and greaves pleats in the shoulder's wainscoting
a knee to the thurible and ankles splayed
across a map of foreign dust how yellow the macramé
the invisibilities of voice the crying and the clarion
that splits blood into uneven hemispheres
how little the perception in the early morning dewfall
lurking shadows and branches weighted with
nocturnal residue not unlike the souls of men
the lettered and the analphabetic the drooping
clientele listing on the borders of a larger water
the depths of an uncanny vowel the stillborn consonant
the epic in the wings of disaster that cannot be borne
the script and totem beast of the assailing drum
fierce the hand still penning clauses though it lacks
fingers to orient the atmospheres to a drill of violins
the aching resonance of breath and the tear-duct
of ancient Spanish prose the peninsular gas and array
of syllabic decay punctuated by the hem and asterisk
that dot the ungodly firmament and much else
there is to mourn this uncounted day among
asphodel and hierophant the loud and roiling
seas that dun the ear with hills of dusky error
phonetic shoots that turn green in rote and wild
the mechanics of women taught in excess to love
the hero in the unmarked grave and do worlds then
come circling in a silent riot to overcome the light
and endless bottoms of sleep's enormous and unformed
continent that lists outside the antiquities of space
and who can read the unraveling text of air
the winds despoiled of passion and ionospheres
that ancient gods deride for their blackened suns
amorphous destinies ! idiolects of gravel !
thunderous daylight the sign and the tomb !

10-18-21

THE GREAT PREPARATION

rest the moonbeams from their wild chase
augment the air with one last breath
thrill the honeycomb ! taste less the sweet
more the bitter as watching leaves fall
the thin blue smoke rising tells it all
magnificent pasts of the seminal vowel
the oriental consonant luxurious and
irretrievable the very difficulties of
packing the small red suitcase with its
hidden music instrument and looms of
memory and situations that never were
the fractions of distance divisible by three
the mummers and guardians of the door
forgetful of their charge sleeping in
the sun's blackened syllable dismantled yet
throbbing in its archaic pronunciation
will it be OK in the shadowy afterthought ?
who will be counted who will be without
number or soul and the lost ticket and
the taxi kept waiting and the surfeit of
desire left diminished on the window sill
how can one know not to turn back ?
cosmetics of the cadaver ! marjoram
and hyacinth a bouquet of forget-me-nots
small animals behind glass poignantly
staring into the other world's fixed
gravity of motion / stasis of passion
the doubled centimeter between sight
and sound the trembling murmur of grass
yearning for darkness and silence

10-19-21

THE LIMITS OF LIGHT

what let off quitting breath the hiatus
of demand and plaintively speaking end
throes of a single throttled sea by its
own lone rock the savaged demeanor
of exile the poet as endeavor and fantasy
falsification of reason turbulent as the day's
eye slowly gyrating around the black homophone
that fixes the sky for its brief eternity
a half-hour spent in ink dissolving alphabets the work
of demons transpired from rock the divulged
deformation of a page of forgotten literature
between two rivers the one of migraine
the other the source of oracles a display
for passion and ambiguity if meaning has
its candle of sense the burning down and out
where once was a city an empire even of mind
what is recognizable as the twin of effort and
disdain educating the hand to move on its own
a decision to reiterate what breath is in the face
of death the evanescent and ever twilight
as hours conclude their sadness and metal
the shining proclivity to leap ignoring
what it says in the furious equivocations
at the end of the paragraph learning to fly
without wings and just hover there above
the lethal surface of documented history
letters of error rumors of script hieroglyphs and
notches wedged into cliff sides to expatiate
on the obsession that angels of doom engender
to read this aright is to mistake purpose for illusion
a sound at a time until resemblance and metaphor
begin to shape words into their uneven hemispheres
a noise and debacle of space for all eons
and frayed by great and enormous anxieties
light transforms itself into a single shimmering sheet
plunged instantly into the loss of time

10-20-21

DEATH IS THE IDENTITY IN THE MIRROR

what face I vow is that I saw looking mirrored
back at me were so many decades in it perceived
the hair gone blank and rugged as a mountainside
the once sleek cheeks the mocking iris deep in
the pitted eye and blind-man's bluff the children's
aim to be as always of a single day the sporting lad
on the chase between the years' cruel illusions
nothing still nothing stays the endless gambit of
dreams and the toss of waking light the losses mount
the foray holds sway at the staring idiom in glass
the lack-luster verbatim of deception's rhetoric
I am forever going to play ! but shadows draw
nigh their mantles darkening the missing hours
and brothers and friends fast disappear like
lightning streaks on the dirty window pane what
achieves the goal of similitude the metaphor and
ampersand's to-and-fro until the calendar has
no more weeks to show in the echo chamber of
the mind and roulette and vagabond symbolize
the repetitions of image and denial the chasms
of mercurial absences where skies withdraw their
infinities leaving azure pock-marked with clouds
incinerated by twilight's curtain call and all this
and more the reflecting dares to tell I confess I
should no more be the same as I ever was but
a difference of others and repercussive ego-play
not me it says written in invisible ink steaming
vapors delusions of charity and hope vanishing
alterations of an unremembered past the signals !
removing the outline efface the postulates ignore
the vicious guttersnipe hiding in sleep's wings
it is Li Po under the bridge looking for his face
in the blackened water's passage to eternity
since the first forbidden draught of canned alcohol
I have been stoned ! and to this very minute scour
the quicksilver surface for its higher truths but
am left as always piercing all remembrance
with death's uncanny disregard for age

10-20-21

THE-FAR-GONE-ONE

this dismay of languages ! tautology and rumor
of phonetic decay and madness they are all babbling
at once piling corpse upon corpse and errors !
to find the rose-apple tree and its shade and there
for an eon to sit without gravity or hind-sight
the world ! a soap bubble ready to burst in a breath
it is not I but the *other* who has fled the Palace
there is no justification for poetry ! navel of the cosmos
erected pillars with inscriptions as to when and how !
liana grass and tangle of metaphors of bliss and loss
the errant mind ! the doubly errant mind !
how much water can a single cupped hand hold ?
the answer is *forever* ! seeking the pathless jungle
the route of indetermination and aphasia
haunted in the left ear by the seductive cooing of Maya
dread-locks and paraphernalia of skin the wardrobe
of reason with combs and eye-liner the heightened virtues
of pornography set in wax for the noontime sun
to excise of its vowels and syllabic structure blackening
cut it all loose ! demand for an unbroken supply chain
for the punctuation of a riddled statecraft when all
that is necessary is an empty head and seclusion
from the ravaging of consonants ! speak no more !
be as the block of unhewn marble in the quarry
the single page is not dominant ! the text is reversible
as are the planets and the course of darkness
nothing is permanent everything is eternal !
silence is the great equivocation ! between one knee
and the other knee are the countless infinities
of sleep the unendurable ! I set off for the dread southland
to avoid those who create temples out of literature
who offend by holding classes expounding on the nature
of noise as if it were the *whole* ! it is the unwholesome and
diseased the very dead in their begging rags the settlers
of the sewer drains and dismissed isotopes with whom
alone I converse in the moment that exists between
illumination and extinction ! behind me are the binomial
universes of human discourse and before me Nothing !
memory is irrelevant and the lotus pond with its fragrances

and the wild birds taking flight because I have whispered
my last utterance ! despond and gratitude the lesser deer
who wander stray and pointless in the Garden ! weeds !
cessation follows cessation

10-21-21

THE DEPARTURE FROM THE PALACE

i

"I want to arrive at the deathless state today"
what am I but an empty sleeve and a begging bowl
averted my gaze from the women tossed into postures
of sleep and distress everything in disarray
ear-rings bracelets jeweled adornments and clasps
clothes awkwardly slipping off shoulder or hip
as if drunk or stunned from excess of lewd acts
mouths agape whites of the eyes staring into the void
saliva and wine and indecent stains the exposed skin
I mount my horse to flee from the surfeits of reason
into an unknown Maze uninhabited but for hungry ghosts
phantoms of linguists or seers apparitions and shadows
still managing to talk using the apparatus of mind
as if it were the force of destiny or an oracle
I put my feet into spurs setting my ears to the keen
wind urgent to become rock or stone the head
an attribute of bone and nothing more ere daylight
capture the error of my departure and the onslaught
begins the net of temptations and recall the variety
of thought untrammeled but for me only to sleep
as grass in the dew and wait for the mowing to start
and beneath the noontime orb suffer heat and by evening
clumps of newly cut grass hemp or weeds tied into bundles
and carried on the shoulders of day-laborers heaved
off into piles by the ditch restless no more still & eternal
but alas and no it is to be pursued and pursue
the unerring path to the deathless mansion
some day far from the mountains of distance and
the waters that surround the source of echoes

and space greater than the light it emanates darkening
remembering that everyone else is like me suffering
the cycle of births for which there is no translation
and once relieved nothing weighs nothing moves
the body a husk the mind a puerile fantasy of noise
and I on my steed somewhere in the universe of memory
the stricken word extinguished lamp unthinking brain
!!!

ii

remembering all else suffer as much or more than I
circling the pit devouring only air the body fails
frail husk dried etymology of desire the blind thrust
off my steed I leap and into the wood tottering go
relieved of the past a weightless burden breath still
assays to work its sport and ill carrying my shoulders
forged spaces between my knees knock the head
against pure stone the other side to see revealing
the lack of difference and the plenitude of rumor
sleep is almost and a dull trance-state interrupted
with echoes of the day before the immense riddle of
remembrance put aside its shapes and disordered thoughts
a murmur a leaf a footfall the grasses of submission
throne of wind-buttresses unassailable garden fragrances
the vitality of sleep buried in the marble ear alone
and I am become redundant at last waiting for the sun's
black voice to strike the crumbling edifice of memory

iii

heaven is in things that do not feel but have beauty
the shape of night or the perfumes of blue and red lotus
the traveler is a weary stone a torn blade of grass
from on high remote asterisks blink puzzling enigmas
the abandoned horse the paragraph full of unspoken words
a mystery on the hill where a lantern has just gone out
bamboo eager to be used as a form of music the mouth
is far and thirsty for plum wine yet nothing more exists
but the scribbled signatures of the departing gods

silence translated into the various languages of the eastern world
the hemispheres beyond the south tremble in their bodies
which are dead and beyond recovery—a mystery is birth
again and again lying here beneath a canopy of autumn leaves
a song that is out of season or wrong
                       a rich silk robe fills
with hastening winds and falls from place useless as ink
drying wordlessly on frayed palm leaves
skin is a metaphor and the panoply of vowels to be memorized
in order to be *forgotten*
life a constant series of separations and grief
the drum is taut the hand learns to tattoo the air
everything is repetition and redundancy
summers come and go in anticipation of the stranger at the door
who can recall the face worn before birth ?
I remember people their various activities
is November upon us ?
masks and pursuits hobbies and vocations
books to tell and lies and subterfuge
the Great year is coming to a close

there is no recovery from oblivion
no penances no atonement can achieve bliss
nodding the head playing the unseen flute
with fingers of grass to become as stone
the Great year is coming to a close

10-25-21

Poetry by Iván Argüelles
published by
Luna Bisonte Prods:

IMMOBILITY [2022]

FIELD HOLLERS (with Solomon Rio) [2021]

TAMAZUNCHALE [2021]

THE SHAPE OF AIR FRAGMENTS [2021]

DIARIO DI UN OTTOGENARIO [2020]

TWILIGHT CANTOS [2019]

CIEN SONETOS [2018]

LAGARTO DE MI CORAZÓN [2018]

FRAGMENTS FROM A GONE WORLD [2017]

LA INTERRUPCIÓN CONVERSACIONAL [2016]

ORPHIC CANTOS [2015]

DUO POEMATA:
ILION—A TRANSCRIPTION
& ALTERTUMSWISSENSCHAFT [2015]

FIAT LUX [2014]

A DAY IN THE SUN [2012]

ULTERIOR VISIONS [2011]

———∾ ∾———

Available at:

https://www.lulu.com/spotlight/lunabisonteprods

or www.spdbooks.org

www.ingramcontent.com/pod-product-compliance
Lightning Source LLC
Chambersburg PA
CBHW030831090426
42737CB00009B/969